Safe Journey

Books in The Artist's Way *Series*

The Artist's Way

Walking in This World

Finding Water

The Complete Artist's Way

The Artist's Way Workbook

The Artist's Way Morning Pages Journal

The Artist's Way Every Day

Other Books on Creativity

The Prosperous Heart

The Writing Diet

The Right to Write

The Sound of Paper

The Vein of Gold

The Artist's Date Book
(illustrated by Elizabeth Cameron Evans)

How to Avoid Making Art (or Anything Else You Enjoy)
(illustrated by Elizabeth Cameron)

Supplies: A Troubleshooting Guide for Creative Difficulties

Inspirations: Meditations from *The Artist's Way*

The Writer's Life: Insights from *The Right to Write*

The Artist's Way at Work
(with Mark Bryan and Catherine Allen)

Money Drunk, Money Sober
(with Mark Bryan)

The Creative Life

Prayer Books

Answered Prayers

Heart Steps

Blessings

Transitions

Prayers to the Great Creator

Books on Spirituality

Prayers from a Nonbeliever

Letters to a Young Artist

God Is No Laughing Matter

God Is Dog Spelled Backwards *(illustrated by Elizabeth Cameron)*

Faith and Will

Memoir

Floor Sample: A Creative Memoir

JEREMY P. TARCHER/PENGUIN

a member of Penguin Group (USA) Inc.

New York

Safe Journey

PRAYERS AND COMFORT FOR
FRIGHTENED FLYERS
AND OTHER ANXIOUS SOULS

Julia Cameron

JEREMY P. TARCHER/PENGUIN
Published by the Penguin Group
Penguin Group (USA) Inc., 375 Hudson Street,
New York, New York 10014, USA

USA · Canada · UK · Ireland · Australia
New Zealand · India · South Africa · China

Penguin Books Ltd, Registered Offices: 80 Strand, London WC2R 0RL, England
For more information about the Penguin Group visit penguin.com

Most Tarcher/Penguin books are available at special quantity discounts for bulk purchase for sales
promotions, premiums, fund-raising, and educational needs. Special books or book excerpts also
can be created to fit specific needs. For details, write Penguin Group (USA) Inc. Special Markets,
375 Hudson Street, New York, NY 10014.

Library of Congress Cataloging-in-Publication Data

Cameron, Julia.
Safe journey : prayers and comfort for frightened fliers and other anxious souls / Julia Cameron.
    p.   cm
ISBN 978-0-399-16183-4
1. Travelers—Prayers and devotions.   2. Air travel—Prayers and devotions.   3. Fear of
flying.   I. Title.
BV283.T7C36   2013   2013001137
204'.33—dc23

Printed in the United States of America
1   3   5   7   9   10   8   6   4   2

Book design by Gretchen Achilles

To my daughter Domenica,

a fearless flyer

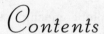

Contents

Safe Journey

Reservations

It's Sunday night. I am due to fly on Wednesday, but already I am anxious. I put my head to the pillow, but there's no sleeping. Instead, I rotisserie with fear. I tell myself to calm down, but it doesn't do any good. In my overactive imagination I am boarding a dangerous flight. I seem to have an endless number of scary scenarios. The pilot can't be trusted. There is too much weight to get safely aloft. The landing gear doesn't work. My mind ticks from one to another. It's midnight, one o'clock, two o'clock. At three a.m., I am still not sleeping. I tell myself, "Julia, you have days before you have to fly. Calm down and sleep." Finally, I drop off, exhausted.

I have told my friends that I am going to be flying

and that I am scared. "Please, pray for me," I have asked them. "I'm flying for business, not pleasure—duty, not beauty." My friends try to reassure me. "You're in my prayers," they say. And, "Flying is really quite safe." They put on their most soothing voices. They talk to me as if I am a small child. Still, I am afraid.

"Be rational," I tell myself, but the fear of flying is not rational. I have read the statistics, and I know that the odds of crashing are very slim. This fact does nothing to soothe me. I have chosen a carrier that advertises the fact that they have the newest fleet. "Is new good?" I catch myself doubting my selection.

IT'S MONDAY, and I am supposed to put in a full day's work. Instead, I put in a day of worry. Every time I look up from my work, I find myself staring into the face of doom. I play and replay the crash that is soon to come. I try to sound normal when I talk with my daughter, Domenica, but she is not fooled. "You're worried about flying, aren't you?" she asks me. Reluctantly, I confess. "Oh, Mommy, I'm sorry you're so scared," my daughter reverses our roles. She is now the older and wiser one.

We make a plan. I will use my cell phone to check in with her right before the flight and right after. I know that her voice will calm me down. "Make believe you're brave and the trick will take you far," I hum Rodgers and Hammerstein's classic song from *The King and I*. Talking to my daughter, I will feign bravery. Enough bravery to get me onto the plane and into my seat. I will talk with her until they tell us to turn off our cell phones. Then I will make a hasty good-bye.

Plan in place with my daughter, I feel calmer—but only a little. I wrap up my day's work and find myself staring at another miserable evening.

Dear God,
Please guide me to
a productive use of my time.
Please give me a hunch
as to what you would have me do.
Amen.

Despite my anxiety, I do not feel I am praying into a void. Instead, I have a sense of communication. I "hear" a response:

Little One,
There is nothing to fear,
you do not need to worry.
I am with you always.
Your worry does not serve you.
Try, instead, to put your fate in my hands.
Allow yourself to let go.
I am always ready to serve you.
I ask you now to relax.

But how to relax? It's several hours before bedtime. I can practice piano for a while, but only for a while. And then what? I call my girlfriend Jennifer Bassey. "Go to the movies," she suggests. "Distract yourself." I take her advice, but the movie I choose is an action adventure film filled with explosions. The explosions do nothing to calm my nerves. I find myself jumpy driving back home. I pilot the car with extra care.

After the movie, it's late and I'm tired. I put myself to bed, dreading another sleepless night. Feeling depressed and desolate, I pray:

Dear God,
Please bring me peace.

Help me to focus on you
as the divine reality.
Give me the grace
to feel your presence.
Guide me and guard me
and allow me to sleep.
Amen.

The prayer calms me. Once more I feel a response:

My Child,
Feel my peace.
I am the great reality.
Feel my presence.
Allow me to guard and guide you.
Gently now,
I bring you sleep.

Mercifully, I fall straight to sleep. Instead of waking up in the night, I sleep straight through.

WINNING WINGS

When we are scared to fly, we can become stuck in worry and find ourselves in a debilitating loop that feels unbreakable. When we are irrationally caught in this cycle of nervous energy, we do well to distract ourselves in any way we can. By shifting our focus away from ourselves, we relieve ourselves of our obsessive fixation on our own fears.

If you are caught in worry, you can try:

Listening to some upbeat music

Doing a crossword puzzle

Watching a movie

Calling a friend "just" to listen

Reading a book for pleasure

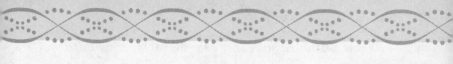

The Eve

When I wake in the morning, it's Tuesday, the day before flying. My peacefulness from the night before has vanished. God feels distant. I do not feel a sense of the divine presence. What I feel now is something close to stark terror. I am too distracted to write and too agitated to pray. This makes me angry. "What are you so scared about?" I demand.

The obvious answer is "death," but is that exactly what I'm afraid of? I've always thought that, faced squarely, there might be some kind of acceptance of death. And yet, I am scared of *something*. When I think about flying, my heart pounds. My pulse races. Make no mistake, I am terrified. Maybe it's the moments just *before* death that scare me. I see the cabin in my mind's eye. I picture all too clearly the terror and chaos. "Why rehearse catastrophe?" I ask myself. Say what I will, my mind spools out scary scenarios.

Once you have tasted flight, you will forever walk the earth with your eyes turned skyward, for there you have been, and there you will always long to return.

—LEONARDO DA VINCI

I call my friend, the actress Jane Cecil, a seasoned optimist.

"Jane, I'm scared of my flight," I confess.

Jane's response is soothing. "Your flight will be fine," she tells me. "I think you might even enjoy it. I get nervous flying from New York to Los Angeles, but I remind myself of all the good reasons I have for going, chief among them how much I will enjoy seeing my sister."

"I don't have anyone I'm eager to see," I tell Jane. "I'm flying in to work with strangers."

"You may like them very much," Jane says. "Don't forget, you told me they seemed nice."

"Did I? I can't remember my optimism."

But Jane assures me I was once optimistic. "I'll stick you in the prayer pot," Jane says. "And don't forget to call me once you land. We'll have dinner when you get here. It will be fine," she repeats.

Jane's optimism does not defeat my pessimism.

Next I call my girlfriend Sonia Choquette. Sonia is a finely tuned psychic. I tell her I am afraid of the flight, and, like Jane, she assures me it will be fine. Surely if disaster were looming, Sonia would spot it but to her eye all is well.

"It's just nerves," Sonia reassures me. "Stage fright. Your nerves are par for the course," she says. "Try to focus on the positive. All will be well."

The reason birds can fly and we can't is simply because they have perfect faith, for to have faith is to have wings.

—J. M. BARRIE, THE LITTLE WHITE BIRD

Hanging up with Sonia, I turn my thoughts resolutely to the good reasons I am making the trip. "It will be an adventure!" I tell myself. There will be sights to see and people to meet. I will earn good money for making the trip. There are students waiting to hear what I will be teaching. I look forward to laying out my toolkit.

It is only when we are suspended in mid-air with no landing in sight that we force our wings to unravel and alas begin our flight . . . but the miracle is in the unfolding of the wings. You may not know where you're going, but you know that so long as you spread your wings, the winds will carry you.

—C. JOYBELL C.

My cheery recitation of the positive reasons for flying doesn't really comfort me. They all seem hollow compared to my fear. My stomach is upset, and I debate driving to the grocery store for saltines. "No. It's just nerves," I decide. I remember that I have half a bottle of ginger ale in the refrigerator. That might do the trick. I pour myself a glass, but it is flat. So much for physical remedies. What I need, I decide, is a spiritual remedy. Tired and overwrought, I find myself cornered into prayer.

> *Dear God,*
> *Set aside my terror. Bring me calm.*
> *Help me to think clearly,*
> *Give me a sense of my next step.*
> *Amen.*

The prayer calms me down. I find myself possessed of a sense of direction. This is an answered prayer. Calmer, I know what I must do. "Ignore your nerves," I tell myself. "It's time to pack."

~~~~~~

If you were born without wings,
do nothing to prevent them from growing.

—COCO CHANEL

~~~~~~

WINNING WINGS

Focus on the positive; remember why you are flying in the first place. Remembering why you have chosen to take the trip can put your feelings of fear into perspective.

Listing three positive reasons for taking the trip can calm your nerves.

For example:

I'm taking this trip because it is part of how I earn my living.

Maybe I will see something—or meet someone—new that I enjoy.

I am looking forward to seeing my friends.

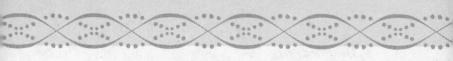

Ready or Not!

Pen in hand, I sit down and start making a list. Pajamas, underwear, extra shirt and slacks, socks, shampoo, toothbrush and toothpaste, passport . . . The list goes on.

I used to pack with no list, often waiting until the morning of my flight to take my suitcase out of the closet. I used the adrenaline of last-minute packing to blot out my fear of the flight. Then there came the trip when my last-minute packing didn't serve me. I forgot several important items. So now packing is done with a list, and it is done the day before. And it is done with a fervent prayer.

Dear God,
Guide my packing.
Let me be thorough.
Help me to remember everything.
Help me to take all I need—
but nothing more.
Amen.

The moment you doubt whether you can fly,
you cease for ever to be able to do it.

—J. M. BARRIE, PETER PAN

The prayer brings me clarity. My list continues: books to teach with, an outline of my teaching agenda, incense, a candle. . . . Item by item, I fill my suitcase—which is looking a little shabby. I tie a red ribbon to the suitcase handle—the better to distinguish it from look-alikes at baggage claim. I go over my list twice to be sure I have everything. Satisfied, I place my suitcase by the door. Now I pack my hand baggage: the book I am reading, the medicines I need to take, a tablet to write on in case I get a sudden brainstorm. With these items packed, I am ready for bed.

~~~~~~

It is beautiful to discover our wings and learn how to fly; flight is a beautiful process. But then to rest on the wings of God as He flies: this is divine.

—C. JOYBELL C.

~~~~~~

I go to bed at nine thirty, but at eleven thirty I am still waiting for sleep. I have set my alarm for dawn. I want time to write my Morning Pages before my ride to the airport shuttle picks me up. At twelve thirty, I resign myself. I will not get enough sleep, and the trip will be made doubly hard. I remember that Jane Cecil once told me that she sometimes thinks fatigue makes doing the mundane things easier. Well, I will certainly have a chance to test that theory out.

WHEN THE ALARM SOUNDS, I am groggy. I slept a total of four and a half hours. I pry myself from bed and make my way to the kitchen where I brew a very strong pot of coffee. Next, I head—cup in hand—to my writing room. I settle into the big leather chair and prop my notebook on the arm. I crawl onto the page, complaining, griping about too little sleep. I write out prayers for myself and my beloveds. It's getting lighter outside.

The morning birds are at the feeders, and I am delighted to spot a flicker—a big, showy bird. Alas, the flicker spots me, too, and sails off to a safer distance. I feel that I am writing uphill this morning. My pages are slow. "I'm scared," I write—and I am scared. Now I am not only scared of the flight, I am also scared I will miss it. I wait impatiently for my ride. We have to drop my dog, Tiger Lily, at the kennel before we rendezvous with the shuttle. Once aboard the shuttle, it is an hour and ten minutes to the airport—that is, if all goes smoothly. I'm hoping that it will. We should miss Albuquerque's rush-hour traffic. We will reach the airport at ten, just after the crush.

~~~~~~

The secret of flight is this: you have to do it immediately,
before your body realizes it is defying the laws.

—MICHAEL CUNNINGHAM

~~~~~~

My ride arrives five minutes early. I barely dressed in time. I stuff my notepad into my briefcase. I got two-thirds of my Morning Pages done. The last page will have to wait until I am standing at the gate. My driver is my neighbor, Rex Oppenheimer. He drives a speedy Mercedes. He knows all the shortcuts. Rex hefts my suitcase into the trunk. I heft Tiger Lily into the backseat. We set off down the mountain.

All journeys eventually end in the same place, home.

—CHRIS GEIGER

At the kennel, there is paperwork to be filled out. Can Tiger Lily have bones? (Yes. Elk bones.) What is the name and number to be called in the event of an emergency? (Elberta Honstein, Española.) Elberta owns a horse farm and is used to dealing with animal emergencies. I trust her to make right decisions in my absence. I race through the forms and bend down to give Tiger Lily a good-bye pat. Back in the car, we speed toward our rendezvous. Rex cuts from one winding street to another.

We make it to Water and Sandoval Streets with ten minutes to spare.

"Did you remember your cell phone?" Rex wants to know. (Yes. It was on my list.)

"I've got it."

"The shuttle bus should be here any minute."

"I'm glad we're early."

"You are nervous."

"Yes. Always."

"But it always goes well!"

"So far."

Rex laughs at my pessimism. He lives sunny-side up. When he travels—and he travels often—he does so with a sense of adventure, even glee. He has been to India, Australia, New Zealand, and virtually all of Europe. He has traveled abroad and lived abroad, spinning great yarns out of his misadventures. I admire his daring. But I cannot emulate it. I wait for the shuttle bus, convinced it will be late.

WINNING WINGS

When we take steps to organize our trip, we take steps to protect ourselves from extra or needless anxiety. Planning ahead gives us a sense of calm control. There are many ways we can plan ahead so that the "day of" goes smoothly.

For example:

A few days before departure, make a list of everything you will pack: clothes, shoes, toiletries, medications, electronics (including chargers!), reading and writing material, passport or photo ID, gifts, etc. As things occur to you, add them to the list. Unhurried, you are less likely to forget something important.

Decide how you will get to the airport. Make your car/shuttle reservation ahead of time and put the confirmation information in your wallet.

Make a list of last-minute things to do,
including printing out your boarding pass,
charging your cell phone, changing the message
on your voice mail, taking out the garbage, etc.

Choose a spot by the door where you will
place everything you need for your trip.

Station your packed suitcase, your purse, your
carry-on, and your travel outfit where you can
find them quickly and easily on the day of the
trip.

The air up there in the clouds is very pure and fine,
bracing and delicious. And why shouldn't it be?—it is
the same the angels breathe.

—MARK TWAIN

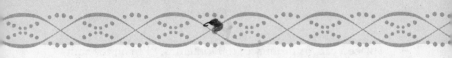

The Shuttle

Right on time, the shuttle bus pulls to the curb. The driver, Frank, swings to the sidewalk. Rex lugs my suitcase from the Mercedes to the bus. Frank consults his clipboard. "Julia Cameron," I tell him. He checks off my name. "You're on American?" I nod. "Yes." He stows my suitcase in the baggage compartment.

"Can I sit up front by you?" I ask.

"Sure," Frank replies.

I kiss Rex good-bye and thank you. Then I scramble up to the shotgun seat. A glance at Frank's clipboard tells me we have a full load. I just hope everyone will be on time.

While the other travelers clamber onto the bus, I

place a call, as promised, to Domenica. "I'm on the shuttle bus," I report when she answers. "I have three hours until my flight leaves. The drive will take only one of them."

"There is a trick to flying. The angels told me." He had smiled at my wide-eyed awe. "You need to forget everything you know as a human being. When you are human, you discover that there is great power in hating the earth. And it can almost make you fly. But it never will." I had frowned, not quite understanding him. "So, what's the trick?"

"Love the sky."

—ANNE FORTIER, JULIET

"You sound pretty good, Mommy," Domenica announces. "Does it feel a little bit like an adventure instead of a catastrophe?"

"The littlest bit," I reply, feigning a courage I do not feel. "I'll call you after I land."

22

Why am I so nervous? Why am I so scared? I have a full hour on the shuttle bus to ponder these questions. Once upon a time I was a fearless traveler. What happened? I have had no flying mishaps. Nothing even close. My fear is irrational and deeply lodged. My sister, Libby, has a fear of flying, and she deals with it by flatly refusing to fly. That doesn't strike me as an option. I want to be brave. I want to be modern. It seems to me my fear of flying must be a fear of something else, something larger. After all, I know that flying is safe. What causes me such apprehension? As the miles of desert roll by outside my window, I think that maybe it is a fear of not being in control. There are many things in life which we cannot control, but flying seems to stand out as the perfect metaphor for all the rest. Perhaps you have a fear of commitment? Flying demands that you commit yourself. Perhaps you have someone, a trusted intimate like I do,

O to speed where there is space enough and
air enough at last!

—WALT WHITMAN

who says blithely, "Yes, when you fly you pretty much agree 'I might just be a fatality.'" Did I agree to any such thing? That remark pretty much defines "tough love." It haunts me as the miles speed past. I pray:

Dear God,
I am afraid to trust you.
I am afraid to relinquish control.
Please give me a sense of safety.
Please let me
place my life in your hands.
Amen.

I find myself thinking of the natural world. The sun and moon follow their carefully orchestrated paths. The stars and planets occupy their proper places, moving in a precise and intricate dance. Seasons come and go with meticulous timing. Surely something large and wonderful planned all of this. This large and wonderful something can surely be trusted.

A sense of calm comes to me, although the shuttle bus hurtles down the highway at 75 mph. We rocket past overstuffed sedans. It's easy to see why flying is said to be safe in comparison to driving, but seat-belted into place, an impending crash seems unlikely. The whole load, all nine of us, is in Frank's hands. He is a good driver, swift but safe. I stare out the window at the desolate desert landscape. It perfectly matches my mood. For miles at a stretch, the terrain looks lunar. It is uninhabited unless you count the sudden appearance of a herd of Indian ponies, so thin they appear spectral, their bones jutting out beneath their hides. How can they forage? What food? Where water? My heart yearns to feed and water them, but we speed on past. Soon the wild ponies are just a memory.

I have a sudden fantasy that once we reach the airport I will scuttle my whole trip and ride back with Frank to Santa Fe. What if I just don't go? What do I stand to lose? There's money to be lost, of course, but there are other things to lose as well: my sense of myself as a competent adult. If I chicken out, I will lose respect for myself. Viewed this way, the trip is a dare—one I must be brave enough to take. No. There's no wriggling out of the flight. Calculating risk, in order to edge myself forward, I have checked the weather and traffic reports. It's not going to rain, but it is a windy day. Windy enough to play with my brave resolve.

As we near the airport, my feelings of dread heighten.

"Is this an intuition?" I ask myself. I remember the stories of 9/11 and the passengers who didn't fly. Trusting their gut, they saved their lives. Is my gut trying to send me a message? Is my dread a premonition? No, I decide. This is just fear I am feeling, not certainty of disaster. If I were a bettor, I would place my money on the flight's safety. Having decided that, I am still afraid. I pray:

> *God, please calm my fear.*
> *Please let me feel your presence.*
> *Help me to trust that you*
> *guard and guide me.*
> *Amen.*

A single sentence comes back to me:

> *All is well.*

Frank takes the exit to the airport. Now we see planes landing. They have made their journey safely. Soon enough mine will be the plane taking off and then, soon enough after that, landing. "It is all routine," I tell myself. "There is nothing to be afraid of." And yet—fear searches for a grip on my stomach lining. I feel the tight

fist of apprehension. Frank pulls up to the curb. My carrier is the first stop. I clamber down from my perch and
thank Frank for the safe trip. It isn't strictly necessary,
but I give him a tip. He thanks me, climbs back into the
driver's seat, and pulls away from the curb.

We swung over the hills and over the town and back
again, and I saw how a man can be master of a craft,
and how a craft can be master of an element. I saw
the alchemy of perspective reduce my world, and all
my other life, to grains in a cup. I learned to watch, to
put my trust in other hands than mine. And I learned
to wander. I learned what every dreaming child needs
to know—that no horizon is so far that you
cannot get above it or beyond it.

—BERYL MARKHAM, WEST WITH THE NIGHT

WINNING WINGS

Once the trip begins, we place our fate in the hands of others. Repeating simple affirmations can help restore a feeling of faith and calm. Try the following, or make up your own.

For example:

"I am safe and secure. There is a great plan for my life. I am on course."

"I trust my driver. I will arrive safely at the airport, in plenty of time."

"I enjoy my journey, and I anticipate my destination."

The Airport

I lug my suitcase to the counter, where a skycap waits.

"Where are you going?" the skycap asks. I give him my destination and my flight number. "You're early," he remarks.

"I know," I answer.

"May I see a photo ID?"

I hand over my passport. He checks it, then hands it back.

"You're checking one bag?"

"Yes."

"That will be twenty-five dollars, and you need to use a credit card."

"Here you go." I pass him my American Express. He

swipes the card and hands it back. Now his computer whirs as it prints out my boarding pass and a receipt for my checked bag.

"You've checked it to New York?" I peel off two crisp bills; the skycap takes them.

"You're all set."

"Thank you, thank you."

"You'll be boarding at gate B-three. But not for an hour and a half."

"Thank you. I like to be early."

"Well, you certainly are. Have a good flight."

"Thank you."

"Good day."

The natural function of the wing is to soar upwards and carry that which is heavy up to the place where dwells the race of gods. More than any other thing that pertains to the body it partakes of the nature of the divine.

—PLATO

Boarding pass in hand, it's onward to security. A clerk asks to see my boarding pass and picture ID. I hand over my passport. He squints at the picture, which admittedly looks nothing like me. He scribbles an okay and I am on my way to the checkpoint. Now it's time to take off coat, shoes, and belt. I place them in a bin. I put my purse and briefcase in another bin. I place my laptop computer in still another bin. Stepping through the scanner, I set off an alarm. I feel a rush of fear adding to my already anxious state. Although I know I'm innocent, I feel guilty.

Why am I a threat? "Step to one side, please." I do so, and a woman pats me down. She discovers I am wearing a pendant. That is what set off the danger signal. Satisfied that I am nonthreatening, she sends me on my way. Paused at a bench, I put on my shoes, belt, and coat. I retrieve my purse, briefcase, and laptop. I head toward my gate. Walking, I pray:

Thank you, God, for getting me safely this far.
Please let me wait calmly
and board without incident.
Amen.

Again I "hear" a response.

Little One,
Why do you doubt my protection?
I am with you always.
There is no need for fear.
Calm yourself.

Despite the soothing message, I am on edge.

~~~~~~

Within all of us is a varying amount of space lint and
stardust, the residue from our creation. Most are too
busy to notice it, and it is stronger in some than others.
It is strongest in those of us who fly and is responsible
for an unconscious, subtle desire to slip into some
wings and try for the elusive boundaries of our origin.

—K. O. ECKLAND

~~~~~~

I settle in to wait. Already, the gate is congested. I
scan my fellow passengers. "Don't be racist," I admonish
myself as my gaze fixes on a dark-complected man. "But
he looks like a terrorist!" my mind persists. "Nonsense!"
I tell myself. "Don't be paranoid."

But I am paranoid. I spot a large man who keeps hitching up his pants. How did he pass security? And the woman who talks so intently and constantly on her cell phone. Is she someone to be trusted? The lounge where I am waiting seems overcrowded. "God, help me," I pray. "Please, God, help me." God does help me. Suddenly I feel steadier. Steady enough to try another prayer.

God, guard and guide me.
Give me a sense of your safety.
Help me feel your protection.
Give the pilot skill.
Give the crew experience.
Allow me to relax.
Let everything go smoothly.
Give me grace and security.
Amen.

I take out my notepad and set myself to finishing my Morning Pages. I no longer feel adversarial. The crowd milling around me feels friendlier. It occurs to me that each traveler has his or her own story. I notice a young woman with blue hair; does she think it looks pretty? What could have possessed her? Will the person meeting her be shocked? Yes, there's a story there. Now I fix my gaze on a man whose carry-on appears to weigh fifty pounds. "What does he have in there?" I wonder, as he hefts it onto his shoulder. "Did he bring his weights with him?" I find myself resenting him. His carry-on seems to me to put the rest of us at risk. How much weight can the plane safely carry? I pray again:

> Lord, bless and protect all of us,
> give us each safety and serenity.
> Help us to enjoy our journey.
> Surround the plane and all the passengers
> with your protective grace.
> Help us to take off, fly and land
> with your power beneath our wings.
> Amen.

Surely God's power is mighty enough to keep our plane safely aloft despite the passenger's heavy bag. I scan the lounge again, and I am relieved to see only two more bulkily laden travelers.

Is it my imagination or do the women staffing the gate now look friendlier? Yes, their smiles seem genuine. They seem to have vast stores of patience to deal with

the travelers' many questions. Watching their exchanges,
I pray:

> God, *thank you for the grace and*
> *good humor of the airplane personnel.*
> *Thank you for their smiles and patience.*
> *Thank you for their calm composure.*
> *Amen.*

"The world is a fascinating place," I tell myself firmly.
I am intrigued by the young woman dressed in a sari. She
has a toddler in tow dressed in Western garb. I speculate
that perhaps it was hard to find small sizes of ethnic wear.
Or maybe her husband is Western and the child's gear is
a nod to his mixed heritage. As I watch, his mother hands
him a pacifier. Clearly she wants him preoccupied, not
acting up. The pacifier does the trick. "Maybe I should
try a pacifier," I think.

What if I were flying to meet a lover rather than flying off to work? Would I be so frightened, or merely excited? I look around the lounge. How many flyers are
heading into welcoming arms? I've little doubt that
makes them calmer. "I would be calmer, too," I tell myself. As it is, my nerves feel like mine alone. Given all

that I know, they strike me as ridiculous. After all, I have flown for years. The fears do nothing but manufacture misery. Why can't I lighten up? I look up and see that the magazine stand is adjacent to a souvenir shop. I notice there are T-shirts in bold New Mexico colors. I am tempted to buy one for myself, but then I think, "No, it will only remind you of your fear."

"Could you save my seat, please?" I ask the person next to me. "I'm going to buy a magazine." I hurry to the newsstand, where I impulsively buy not one but five magazines, three of them tabloids. "Thank you," I say to the Good Samaritan who held my seat. I settle in to read a tabloid. Its pages are full of mayhem and infidelity. By comparison, my own life is dull, thankfully.

Dear God, thank you for my life's serenity.
Amen.

My soul is in the sky.

—WILLIAM SHAKESPEARE

I notice more airport personnel milling around behind a long desk full of computers. That tall man in uniform must be our pilot. His face looks flushed. Could he be a drinker? I want to ask someone, but who? Both of the women behind the counter now look crabby. Someone must have annoyed them. I will ask for a new seat assignment. That gives me a legitimate excuse for closer inspection. As I step toward the desk, a short, stocky man in uniform greets the pilot. He is our copilot. I am relieved. He looks friendly and competent. "Thank you, God," I breathe. I'm given a new seat, farther forward in the cabin. A gaggle of flight attendants arrives next. They are weathered, and two of them are plump. Clearly, they are veterans.

It's time to board. We are boarding by section. I gather my magazines and my carry-on bag. My section is next. Yes, my carry-on bag fits the "bag sizer." Relieved, I make my way forward, showing my boarding pass. Now I am at the jetway. The crowd presses forward. "What if we all die together?" my mind proposes. I replay stories of entire sports teams being wiped out. "Stop it!" I insist, mentally tallying the crowd for its diversity. There is a woman with a babe in her arms. This makes me feel safer. Surely, God wouldn't kill a baby.

Julia Cameron

WINNING WINGS

When we focus our attention outside ourselves, we are reminded that we are not the only ones hoping to get safely to our destination. Dozens, hundreds, thousands—millions of people have the faith to fly. Taking the attention off ourselves, we experience a sense of companionship.

Look around the airport. Allow yourself to people-watch. Imagine what other people's stories are, from the person working at the gate to the many varied travelers. See if thinking about others lessens your anxiety about yourself.

You haven't seen a tree until you've seen
its shadow from the sky.

—AMELIA EARHART

All Aboard

I near my row.

Please, God,
Let me have pleasant traveling companions.
Let me settle comfortably in my seat.
Let me enjoy this flight.
Amen.

I do have an aisle. Settling in, I remember to turn off my cell phone. The flight attendant makes the announcement about switching off all electronic devices. I check my computer: off.

"I don't really think that computers interfere," comments my neighbor. "Still, just in case, eh?"

"Just in case," I echo.

~~~~~~

Flyers feel a certain kinship with the sight of the earth
unencrusted by humanity, they want to see it that way in
one sweeping view, in reassurance that nature still exists
on her own, without a chain-link fence to hold her.

—RICHARD BACH

~~~~~~

But what if computers do interfere and a rebellious traveler leaves his switched on? Would we manage to take off only to have the "interference" send us hurtling back to earth? It's a scary scenario. Perhaps all the other passengers also have this montage unspooling in their minds. Obedient, they turn their computers off. I try to trust that no one will flaunt the rules. It occurs to me that flying requires faith—not only faith in our pilot but faith in our fellow travelers as well. We are traveling together with the tacit understanding that no one will fling open an exit door, sucking us out into space.

But what's this? The plane shudders—once, twice, a third time. The pilot's voice comes over the intercom. "This is your captain. Please move to your seats quickly. Right now we have a wind of forty-one knots. If it gets up to fifty knots, we cannot fly. Please take your seats swiftly and we will get under way. Expect turbulence until we reach ten thousand feet."

〰〰〰〰〰〰〰〰〰〰〰〰〰〰〰〰〰〰〰〰〰〰

Man must rise above the Earth—to the top of the atmosphere and beyond—for only thus will he fully understand the world in which he lives.

—SOCRATES

〰〰〰〰〰〰〰〰〰〰〰〰〰〰〰〰〰〰〰〰〰〰

"Oh, great," mutters the traveler in the window seat. "I hate turbulence."

"We all do," I say. The plane shudders again as it backs away from the gate.

"I wonder how many knots we are at now?" remarks the middle-seat traveler.

"He won't fly if it's too dangerous," I hear myself say soothingly. The plane shudders yet again as it starts to taxi into position for takeoff. "We must be close to fifty knots," I catch myself thinking. The plane picks up speed. Soon it hurtles down the runway. I find myself feeling a mixture of fear and excitement. There is something romantic about being one amid a crowd of strangers. All of us have taken the leap of faith necessary for flying. Collectively we have decided to trust our pilot. Perhaps his flush is just sunburn, I speculate. Yes, that is a more comforting thought. As the plane takes off into the wind, I quickly pray:

Dear God, please keep us safe.
Please guide our pilot.

I repeat it like a mantra.

Dear God, please keep us safe.
Please guide our pilot.

Just as promised, we hit turbulence. The plane bucks and bounces.

Dear God, please keep us safe.
Please guide our pilot.

"I hate this. I hate this," mutters the window-seat flyer.

"Me, too," joins the middle-seat flyer.

"It will be over soon," I tell them and myself. How calm I am able to sound! I deserve an Oscar. I find myself wanting to be a source of comfort to my companions. I try to soothe them just as my friends tried to soothe me.

"GOD, HELP US!" I add under my breath. I am trying to practice a spiritual slogan, "Let go and let God." I want to let go of my apprehension and trust God to guard and guide us.

Dear God, please let me trust you!
Amen.

Unexpectedly, I find myself believing in the skills of our pilot. And surely he must pray as well.

God, thank you for helping our pilot.
Thank you for keeping us safe despite the turbulence.
Please cushion our choppy flight.
Thank you for your help.
Amen.

43

The plane continues to buck and drop. I feel calm despite the turbulence, but then my brief moment of faith evaporates. I feel a surge of anxiety, something close to panic. How long can I tolerate the choppy air? Not much longer. I remember the pilot's promise of smooth air at 10,000 feet. I pray again:

> *God, please guide us to smooth air.*
> *Please let us reach 10,000 feet.*
> *Please, please, end this turbulence.*
> *Quiet my nerves and give me faith.*
> *Thank you for your help.*
> *Amen.*

This time it appears my prayer is answered. The turbulence stops. Blessedly smooth air takes its place. I catch myself sighing. I "hear" a soothing message:

> *Little One, all is well.*
> *Why do you doubt my protection?*
> *I watch over you with care.*

"Thank God that's over," says the window-seat passenger.

"On cargo flights, they stay in the turbulence," the middle-seat traveler volunteers. "They don't change altitudes. That's just for us."

"How did you hear that?" I ask.

"My brother-in-law is a pilot," comes the reply. "He's full of stories about how safe it is."

"Really?"

"Really. He thinks it's hilarious that I'm frightened."

"I don't think it's funny."

"Me neither."

Just for a beat, I relax. My neighbor is as frightened as I am—a kindred spirit.

I feel our shared fear bonds us somehow. Just for a moment I appreciate the beauty of all of us strangers sitting so close to one another. Comforted, I settle in for the long flight.

~~~~~~

There is no sport equal to that which aviators
enjoy while being carried through the air
on great white wings.

—WILBUR WRIGHT

~~~~~~

WINNING WINGS

Being willing to pray when we are scared, we admit our own powerlessness and, thus, invite the help of a higher power. It is the paradox of prayer that when we admit our own limitations we become more powerful, as we are now willing to accept help.

Try saying a prayer to yourself. You can say it in your mind, write it out, whisper it to the window. Allow yourself as you pray to imagine that your prayer has *already* been answered, and allow yourself to feel the feelings that would go along with that answered prayer.

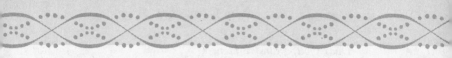

Misery Loves Company

I've brought my computer, and I could be virtuous, but instead of work I turn to my tabloids. There is an entire issue devoted to plastic surgery gone awry. There are before and after shots of many celebrities. They look better before their surgical "improvements." Abruptly, I feel the plane lurch.

Suddenly, the seat-belt sign flashes on. The captain's voice slices the air: "This is your captain speaking. We have encountered some unexpected turbulence. Return to your seat and fasten your seat belt." I am in my seat with my seat belt fastened. When the plane bucks again, I am prepared.

Dear God, I am frightened.
Please let us find smooth air again.
Get us out of this turbulence.
Thank you for your help.
Amen.

My prayer is grounding. Again, the sentence comes to me:

Little One, all is well.

～～～～～～～～～～～～～～～～～～～～～～～～～～

Pilots are a rare kind of human. They leave the
ordinary surface of the world, to purify their soul in
the sky, and they come down to earth, only after
receiving the communion of the infinite.

—JOSÉ MARÍA VELASCO IBARRA

～～～～～～～～～～～～～～～～～～～～～～～～～～

As abruptly as it began, the turbulence ends. The captain keeps the seat-belt sign lit, but the flight attendants move down the aisle, serving beverages. Both of my seatmates ask for alcohol. One orders a double martini. The other asks for a double scotch on the rocks. "I'll have a tomato juice."

"We don't have tomato juice, but I can give you Bloody Mary mix," the flight attendant offers. I accept.

"Don't you want a *drink* drink?" my neighbor inquires.

"No. I'm fine."

"I always drink when there's turbulence."

"Ah."

The flight attendant moves on down the aisle. I turn again to my tabloids. The *National Enquirer* features a story of Hollywood divorce. The cause? Infidelity. My heart goes out to the hapless celebrity who was cuckolded. Fame is no protection against human pain. I read the story, grateful that it isn't me. The gossip rags do their job, distracting me from my fear of flying. Cocooned by trivia, I now enjoy a calm, peaceful flight. I fold my tabloids in my lap and close my eyes. I have brought a neck pillow and hope to doze off, but no such luck. Five, ten, fifteen minutes pass, and I feel the return of anxiety. My breath shortens, my pulse pounds. I grip the armrest. What causes my fear? It seems to come not from facts but from the fictions my overactive imagination conjures up.

"I'm afraid because I am not in control," I remember. There are many things I can't control in my life, but flying is the truly obvious one. I have placed my life in the pilot's hands, and I try to let go. No such luck. I try another prayer:

> *Dear God, please help our pilot.*
> *Please help me trust his wisdom and skill.*
> *Please help me to let go.*
> *Let our flight be smooth and uneventful.*
> *Let us land without mishaps.*
> *Amen.*

Flying is an act of faith. Whether or not you trust your pilot, you can always try to trust God. I try to visualize God's hands beneath the wings. Especially on take-off and landing, I pray:

> *God, put your hands beneath our wings.*
> *God, give us safety.*
> *God, bear us to our destination.*
> *Amen.*

But now, despite my prayers, my mind races from fear to fear. I think about my baggage. Will it make the trip safely? Was it loaded onto the right plane or is it flying halfway around the world in the opposite direction? I will find out at baggage claim, when I spot the bright red ribbon. If all goes well, my bag will contain everything that I need. After all, I made a list and executed it item by item. Extra socks. Extra underwear. Deodorant. I remember I was careful to pack my prescriptions in my hand baggage. If my suitcase gets lost, at least I will have my medicines, if not my clothes. There is a defensive wisdom in how I pack. All liquids are packed in Ziploc plastic bags. My shampoo cannot leak, spoiling my clothing. I remembered to pack contact lens solution and an extra set of lenses. I remember that I prayed while packing, and I try to trust that all is well.

The flight attendant is back at our row, offering a second round of drinks. My seatmates repeat their martini and scotch on the rocks. I repeat my Bloody Mary mix. This time the flight attendant offers me peanuts. I ask if there's a larger snack, and for five dollars I purchase cheese and crackers, raisins, and nuts. One slice of cheese and two crackers, a skimpy amount. "Next time," I vow, "I will pack my own food." I debate asking for a second round of cheese and crackers, but balk at spending ten dollars. Bad enough I paid twenty-five dollars to check my bag; my bargain flight is getting to be expensive. I pray to be satisfied:

> *Dear God,*
> *Help me to enjoy my snack.*
> *Help it to be "enough."*
> *Please take the edge off my hunger.*
> *Help me to be satisfied.*
> *Thank you.*
> *Amen.*

I turn back to my tabloids. The cover story asks the question "How did Natalie Wood really die?" The answer, to be blunt, is she drowned. But the tabloid hints at foul play. And was she having an affair with Christopher Walken, who was also on board? Her husband was jealous and suspicious. Even at the remove of more than a quarter century, the facts remain compelling. Natalie Wood's death remains an enigma. The "new" facts prove to be just a rehashing of old speculation. Disgruntled, I fold up my tabloid. I feel a wave of self-directed anger.

I'm so gullible! The tabloids seldom deliver on their lurid headlines.

"If you're finished with that, I'd like to see it," my middle seatmate pipes up.

"I'm done," I say, handing over the tabloid.

"I never have the nerve to buy this."

"It keeps my mind off the flight," I volunteer.

"Anything that does that can't be all bad. Computer games, an iPod, a new book on Kindle, I've got all of them."

"So you're scared, too?" I think I know the answer.

"That's why I drink. Two double scotches, and I don't care if we crash."

"That's why I guzzle martinis," chimes in the window-seat passenger.

"So we've got three scaredy-cats in a row," I say. Then I pray silently to myself:

Dear God,
Thank you for our candor.
Thank you for our shared humanity.
I'm grateful that I'm not alone
in my fear and apprehension.

Thank you for giving me courage
to admit my fears.
I open my fearful heart
to your soothing grace.
Thank you for my comfort.
Amen.

As I pray, I feel my fear lifting. And so I pray again:

Dear Lord,
Please help my seatmates
to find faith in your protection.
Help us, all three,
to trust your loving kindess.
Thank you for my growing trust.
I appreciate the skill with which
you inspire our pilot and crew.
Amen.

I sense an answered prayer. Once more, the Higher Power seems to be addressing me as tenderly as a child:

Little One,
I bless all my children.

I guard, guide, and protect all three of you.
Thank you for your growing trust.

The pilot's voice announces, "Your flight attendants will be passing down the aisle, collecting trash."

A light tap on my shoulder, and my eyes blink open. It is the flight attendant, saying, "I'll take your glass now."

I hand over my empty glass. My seatmates do the same. I crinkle up the wrapping to my cheese and crackers. "Here you go," I say, handing the crumpled ball to the flight attendant, who snags it into a trash bag.

"Thank you." She moves on down the aisle.

I've got one more tabloid to go, this one focusing on celebrity weight loss. There are pictures of celebrity cellulite, inviting us to guess whose cellulite is whose. Some of the ripples belong to people I've never heard of, television celebrities. I remember my cheese and crackers. Would they cause cellulite? I hope not.

Dear Lord,
Thank you for my snack.
May my body use it wisely.
May I have no cellulite.
Amen.

Julia Cameron

WINNING WINGS

Remembering that we are not alone in our struggles, we open ourselves to feelings of camaraderie and connection. Allowing ourselves to indulge in reading that might not be our norm, we are allowing ourselves an earned distraction from our own discomfort. Tabloids discussing other people's woes at length can be strangely comforting and often riveting.

Allow yourself to buy tabloids, and allow yourself to indulge in them on your flight. This is mind candy you would otherwise never eat.

Gliders, sailplanes, they are wonderful flying machines. It's the closest you can come to being a bird.

—NEIL ARMSTRONG

A Wing and a Prayer

Excuse me." My middle seatmate taps my arm.

"Yes?"

"When you close your eyes, what are you doing?"

The question catches me off guard.

"What am I doing?" I echo.

"Yes, you sit so still."

"Ah." I decide to be open. What do I have to lose? "I'm praying," I say.

"I thought you might be praying!"

"It calms me down."

"It must be nice." My seatmate sounds wistful.

"What?"

"Being a believer. If I were a believer, I wouldn't need scotch." My seatmate sounds rueful. Also a little bit tipsy. Four shots' worth.

"No, I suppose not."

"Tell me a prayer. All I can think of is, 'God, help me!'"

"That's a fine prayer," I reply.

"Well, it's to the point." My seatmate sounds good-humored.

"Candor is good; I'm sure God likes it," I say.

"I don't know what God likes," my seatmate confesses.

"I think honesty."

"Well, then I honestly don't know what God likes." The two of us laugh. This conversation trumps the tabloids.

No one can realize how substantial the air is,
until he feels its supporting power beneath him.
It inspires confidence at once.

—OTTO LILIENTHAL

"I ask for protection," I volunteer.

"That's a good one."

"And I say, 'Thank you.'"

"For what?"

"For God's protection."

"You mean you just assume your prayer is answered?"

"Yes. I think God likes to answer prayers." My seat-mate mulls this over. I turn back to the tabloids. Before long, I hear:

Little One,
Your faith is contagious.

~~~~~~

It's wonderful to climb the liquid mountains of the sky.
Behind me and before me is God and I have no fears.

—HELEN KELLER

~~~~~~

"You just assume you'll get a positive response?" My seatmate worries this question like a bone.

"I think God likes it when we pray."

"So you pray about everything?"

"Well, I did just pray, 'Dear God, please don't give me cellulite.'"

"You did?"

"Yes, actually, I did." The two of us laugh again. I catch my breath and find myself praying:

Dear God,
Thanks for our rapport.
Amen.

"There, you did it again. You closed your eyes and you prayed."

"Yes, I did. I said, 'Thanks for our rapport.'"

There is a moment of silence while my neighbor mulls over what I've said.

"It's nice. I mean, you don't seem like a fanatic or anything," my neighbor finally pronounces.

"And you're a gentle skeptic."

"Thank you, I think. Now are you asking God for patience with your pushy seatmate?"

"I've enjoyed our conversation."

"Let me ask you one last thing."

"Should I brace myself?"

"Do you feel guided?"

"That's a tricky question. I would say I feel guided in retrospect. I don't always feel guided in the moment. But, as it turns out, God's always got my back."

"So you feel God's a friend?"

"Yes, I feel loved."

"That would be wonderful—I'll let you read now." With that, my neighbor turns away. I pick up my tabloid, but my focus is still on my neighbor's words. Almost automatically, I pray:

Dear God,
Thank you for our intimacy.
Thank you for knowing my secret heart.
Please give my seatmate a sense of your presence.
Please be a friend.
Amen.

My seatmate snags my sleeve.

"Stop praying; teach me to pray!"

"Try a simple prayer," I suggest.

"Under the circumstances, I'd say a really simple prayer—'Help!'"

"That's perfect. Now say, 'Thank you, thank you for your help.'"

"Thank you for your help."

"That's all there is to it."

"Really?"

"Really."

"I do feel calmer."

"Good." Tutoring my seatmate, I find myself feeling calmer, too. I feel a sense of faith that all is well. I think of the spiritual axiom "You have to give it away to keep it," "it" being faith in this case. If God is right that faith is contagious, my neighbor has caught something. I pray:

Thank you, God, for the gift of faith—
mine and my neighbor's.
Thank you for my reliance on you.
Thank you for my trust in your interest.
Thank you for my beliefs that you hear my prayers.
As to flying, thank you for releasing my fear.
I enjoy your powerful protection.
Grant me safety and
gratitude for your care.
Amen.

My prayer seems to build a bridge from me to God. I feel momentarily secure. Trusting God's protection,

my attention flickers to my fellow travelers. I pray for
them:

Dear God,
Please bless my rowmates.
Let them feel your presence.
Let them know your answered prayers.
Give them faith in your protection.
Allow them to feel your safety.
Amen.

My middle seatmate has scrunched eyes, tightly shut.
I can feel concentration. I tap the armrest.

"I'm praying," my seatmate blurts.

"It doesn't need to be so hard," I say.

"I'm trying to get God's attention."

"You've already got God's attention."

"Really?"

"Yes, really. A prayer is a simple request. You don't
force God to answer."

"I guess I was using force."

"It's not necessary. Try assuming that God is recep-
tive, maybe even eager to respond to you."

"Maybe you should pray for me."

"I did."

"Maybe you could do it again?"

"All right." And so I pray aloud in a whisper:

Dear God,
Please hear our prayer.
Please honor our request for safety.
Please give us your protection.
Thank you for your guidance
and your guardianship.
Please bless our pilot with your wisdom.
Let us fly safely and land safely.
Amen.

My seatmate visibly relaxes. My prayer hit the right note, evidently.

"I feel much better," my seatmate says.

"I'm glad," I reply. And I *am* glad.

"You make it seem so simple."

"But it is simple."

"To you it is."

"God isn't distant and foreboding, God is right with us, waiting for our prayer."

"I wish I believed."

"Act as if you believe. Soon enough you will."

"There you go again, making it simple."

"But it is."

"Pray again, would you?"

"A simple prayer?"

"Yes."

So again, I pray:

Dear God,
Please make our path to you plain, direct, and simple.
Please meet us halfway.
Thank you for your gift of contact.
Help us to feel your presence now and always.
Amen.

"You make prayer seem so natural."

"It is natural; try it again."

"Me?"

"Just give it a shot."

My seatmate sits up straighter then leans in my direction and whispers:

Dear God,
Please hear my prayer.

I ask you for contact.
Let me feel your presence.
Give me safety and protection.
Give me faith.
Amen.

"That was great!" I exclaim. My seatmate acts embarrassed. The window-seat traveler is very quiet. I wonder if our prayers are being eavesdropped upon.

"I just copied you," my neighbor volunteers.

"It was still great. How do you feel?"

"The same. No, a little foolish. No, maybe a little bit better."

"Then that's an answered prayer."

"How do you know it's not just your imagination?"

"Keep it up. You'll find it feels steady. Try this prayer:"

Dear God,
Thank you for your contact.
Thank you for your protection.
Help me to know you are real.
Amen.

"You don't worry about tact? I mean, God might be insulted by 'Help me to know you are real.'"

"I worry more about candor than about tact. God already knows the truth of how I feel. There's no point pretending otherwise."

"You pray about anything and everything?"

"Yes, I guess I do. God is my catcher's mitt. There's nothing too wild to be caught."

"I like that idea that prayer is like a pitch. I bet I could throw one over the plate."

"I bet you could."

Now I relax, feeling a wonderful sense of camaraderie. My neighbor's prayers have reinforced my own. I sense a benevolent something cradling my neighbor and myself. I pray:

Dear God,
Thank you for your presence.
Thank you for letting me feel you near.
Thank you for keeping your promise
that wherever two or more are gathered together
there you are in our midst.
Amen.

WINNING WINGS

You do not have to know who or what God is to pray. Imagine what you might *like* God to be—a friendly grandfather, a waterfall, or a wise Yoda-like figure—and then pray to that. You need not even use the word "God" to connect to something higher. Simply think of *Something* that you can believe in as a positive, guiding force and ask this Something for its comfort and guidance. As foreign as this may feel, it is worth a try. Pray and then pause. You may feel a contact. It is often surprising how immediate that source of optimism actually seems to be when we are willing to reach for it.

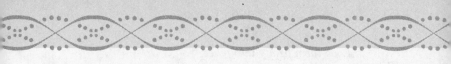

Landing

I no sooner finish my prayer than my neighbor nudges me.

"I'm worried about landing."

"The gears worked on takeoff," I say. "I'll bet they'll work again now."

"How can you be so sure?" My neighbor is asking for reassurance.

"We'd better pray. Here we go," I say. My tone is calm.

Dear God,
Please give us a safe landing.
Please see that the gears work smoothly.

Lock them firmly into place.
Let us hear the mechanisms working.
Let us trust the hydraulics.
Bless our ears.
Amen.

My neighbor laughs. "That was a good prayer. I like the line about 'bless our ears.'"

~~~~~~

Aeronautics was neither an industry nor a science.
It was a miracle.

—IGOR SIKORSKY

~~~~~~

"Well, if we trust our ears, we'll know that we are safe as the gears grind into place."

"I never thought of it that way. I'm always startled by the noise."

"So this time expect it. It's a good sound."

"If you say so."

"I do."

My neighbor is quiet for a long moment. Then comes a confession: "You help me a lot."

"I'm glad, but I think you're helping yourself, or God's helping you, or both."

"The real test will be when I fly home. If we don't crash now, that is."

"We're not going to crash."

"You're certain?"

"I'm certain."

"What if it's God's will that we crash?"

"Well, then I would try to be okay with that."

"How could you be?"

"I'd try to feel that I'd lived fully, that it was enough."

"Maybe that's why I feel so afraid. I don't feel that I've lived fully. I don't feel that it is enough."

This confession moves me. It occurs to me that a fear of dying is directly tied to the feeling of not having lived fully.

"Give me your hand; don't be shy." My neighbor offers me a hand. I pray aloud:

Dear God,
Please grant me peace.

Help me to know that I have lived enough.
Help me to live more fully in the future.
Give me knowledge of your will for me
and the power to carry that out.
Help me to trust your benevolence.
Let me have faith in your guardianship,
faith enough in your goodwill.
Thank you, God, for hearing me.
Amen.

My neighbor takes back the hand.

"Better?" I ask.

"Better."

A high-pitched bell dings. It is the captain speaking. "Ladies and gentlemen, I have turned on the seat-belt sign. We are beginning our final descent. Please return to your seats and make sure your seat belts are securely fastened."

My seat belt is fastened snugly, but I give it a little tug. My neighbor's seat belt dangles loose.

"Your seat belt," I say.

"I don't use them," my neighbor responds.

"But why?"

"I can get out faster."

"I suppose that's true."

The plane banks sharply to the left. I find myself staring down at the twinkling lights below. My neighbor clutches my arm. Suddenly there is the grinding noise of the landing gear locking into place.

"It's okay," I say, feeling a little queasy. The plane rights itself, settling down for its approach. I look out the window. The ground below looms close. We are flying over superhighways, then over warehouses and hangars. The lights for the landing strip appear below. They speed past as we skim closer to the ground. Then, with a lurch, we make contact. The captain brakes, firing the jets in reverse. The plane slows.

"We made it!" I say.

"We made it," my neighbor echoes. I close my eyes and pray:

Thank you, God, for our safe journey.
Thank you for our landing.
Amen.

"You're praying again, aren't you?" my neighbor asks.

"I'm just saying thanks."

"I should say thanks, too."

"Go ahead."

Thank you, God.
Amen.

~~~~~~

> He rode upon a cherub, and did fly: yea, he did fly
> upon the wings of the wind.
>
> —OLD TESTAMENT: PSALMS XVIII, 10, C. 150 BCE

~~~~~~

"There we go." I smile at my neighbor. "Safe and sound!"

"I've just been eavesdropping," pipes up the window-seat traveler. "I've been silently piggybacking on your prayers."

"You mean our whole row has been praying?" my neighbor asks.

"Yes, and here we are, safe and sound," I announce.

"Next time I fly, I'll skip the martinis."

"And I'll skip the scotch." Both of my neighbors are smiling.

"Next time I fly, I'll think of you," I say.

I punch my daughter's phone number into the cell phone. She answers on the second ring. "You made it."

"Yes, it was bumpy, but I'm here."

"You sound calmer."

"Yes, I had good seatmates. That always helps."

My seatmate is listening to my call. "Glad to be of service!" I hang up. "Good you have someone to call."

"It's my daughter. She worries about my worry."

A flight attendant's voice comes on the air: "Please remain in your seats with your seat belts securely fastened until the plane arrives at the gate."

"They take every precaution," I say. "They don't want a stampede."

"Who wants to be trampled?" asks the window-seat traveler.

The captain's voice cuts the air: "This is your captain. We realize you had your choice of carriers, and we want to thank you for choosing to fly with us. Your seat-belt sign is turned off, and you are free to move about the cabin."

"Ah, here we go." I turn to my neighbors. "Well, it was a pleasure—that is, you, not the flight."

"Back at you!"

WINNING WINGS

Being kind to others can give us a sense of groundedness and optimism. Choose one person whom you can help in some small way. Perhaps you can help the elderly woman retrieve her suitcase, or allow the young and overwhelmed mother to cut you in line. It may be a tiny gesture, but allow yourself to be generous with one of your travel companions and see if you don't feel a little better yourself.

Don't let the fear of falling keep you from
knowing the joy of flight.

—LANE WALLACE

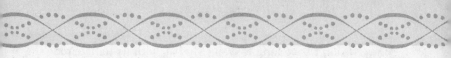

Journey's End

We press forward through the jetway. I'm alert for the baggage-claim sign, still nervous about my luggage. Our bags are coming in on carousel 3. I hurry toward the carousel, apprehensive. I reach it before the bags. I position myself where I can clearly see the bags tumbling out and can quickly grab mine. I pray:

Dear God,
Please let my bag arrive safely.
Please let the systems work.
Please let me spot my bag easily.
Amen.

I don't have long to wait. My bag with its telltale red ribbon tumbles down the chute. I snag it and make my way to the taxi line. The line is moving briskly, and I don't have long to wait. I step to the curb. The taxi driver hoists my luggage, and I give him the address I am going to.

"Sure thing," he says.

~~~~~~

I ask people who don't fly, "How can you not fly when you live in a time in history when you can fly?"

—WILLIAM LANGEWIESCHE

~~~~~~

I settle into the back of the cab. A wave of relief washes over me. I've safely made it. My cab driver is talkative.

"How was your flight?" he wants to know.

"Bumpy," I tell him. "There was turbulence."

"That's too bad."

"But my neighbors were nice."

"That helps. You were safer in the air than you are in this taxi."

"Don't spook me."

"It's just the facts."

My cell phone rings. I answer it. Domenica's voice is on the line. "Are you in a taxi? Did you get your bag okay?"

"Yes on both counts."

"You know, you were safer in the air than you are in that cab."

"So I'm told. I've got my seat belt on, but traveling by car doesn't really scare me."

"I'm glad you're safe and sounding calmer."

"Thanks for the call."

"Oh, you're welcome."

"Family checking up on you?" asks the driver as I hang up.

"Yes, I have a fear of flying."

~~~~~~

I cannot imagine anyone looking at the
sky and denying God.

—ABRAHAM LINCOLN

~~~~~~

"A lot of people do. I get to hear all about it."

"I don't know what to do about it except pray."

"Yes, well, that's probably the best thing to do."

"I could pray now."

Thank you, God,
for my understanding cabbie.
Amen.

~~~~~~

You are brave. Not brave because you are going to
be facing any physical dangers; you are not really
going to. I mean brave in another, deeper sense.
By being on this flight you have shown that you
are willing to explore your own identity to
discover what might lie within you.

—HARRY BAUER

~~~~~~

The cabbie chuckles. I remember that I promised
Jane I would call her upon landing.

"Welcome, Julia," Jane greets me. "You're safe and
sound?"

"Yes, I made it. The flight wasn't so bad, although we had turbulence at the beginning."

"But after that it was fine?" Jane persists optimistically.

"Yes," I tell her. "All's well."

"Of course it is. I was praying."

"And I was praying, too."

"I'm so happy it all went well. So get a good night's sleep and I'll see you tomorrow. How does dinner at Pascalou at five-thirty sound?"

"Perfect. I've got a lunch with Gerard. Bye-bye!"

The cabbie drops me at my hotel. I check in without incident. I am no longer expecting the worst. I am back to being a competent adult. I have a full week before I am due to travel back. I am determined to put my future air travel out of mind. I will focus on my teaching and the new people that I will meet. There is no point in letting needless trepidation spoil my stay.

WINNING WINGS

After everything has "all worked out okay," we often forget to be consciously grateful. Take a moment to make a small gratitude list.

For example:

I am grateful that I arrived safely.

I am grateful for my comfortable hotel.

I am grateful that my daughter is happy.

I am grateful for the pleasant weather.

I am grateful for my carefully packed luggage.

Oh! "darkly, deeply, beautifully blue,"
As someone somewhere sings about the sky.

—GEORGE GORDON BYRON, DON JUAN, IV. 110

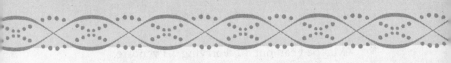

The Destination

There's no point in letting needless trepidation spoil my stay," I announce to my friend Gerard when we rendezvous for lunch.

"Excellent thinking," Gerard says. Gerard is level-headed. When I tell him I am afraid to fly, he tells me how safe flying is. He suggests I Google airline safety. Better yet, he Googles it for me and comes up with reassuring statistics. "So don't waste your energy worrying," he concludes as we place our order.

"Oh, Gerard, I know it isn't rational," I tell him.

"It's not—so just cut it out," he urges.

"I wish it were that simple," I say.

"It is simple. Don't make it complicated," he chides.

"Maybe I can put off worrying," I venture.

"That's the idea!" Gerard praises my return to sanity. "Before every flight, put off worrying a little longer and then a little longer, and one day, *pfft!* You'll forget to worry entirely."

I try to imagine Gerard's scenario. What if—*pfft*—I forgot to worry? Was such a thing even possible? Gerard assures me that it is. I make a dinner date with him for the last night before flying back home.

"So try to put off worrying until then," he urges.

"Okay, I'll try to put off worrying."

When Gerard and I wrap up lunch, I have three hours to kill before meeting with Jane. I decide to go to the Metropolitan Museum of Art, to my favorite section: the Asian wing. Once there, I am struck by the timelessness of the serene Buddhas.

Whenever the thought of flying crosses my mind, I brush it aside. "You can worry later," I tell myself. To my surprise, this strategy seems to work. I pass two hours without worry. Gerard's postponement strategy is working. Freed from anxiety, my mind focuses on the here and now. I enjoy the walk from the museum to Pascalou, the French bistro where I am meeting Jane.

"How are you doing with your fear?" she asks me.

"Better," I reply.

"That's an answered prayer," Jane remarks.

I tell her about Gerard's postponement stratagem.

"God speaks to us through people," Jane says.

~~~~~~

Whether outwardly or inwardly, whether in space or time, the farther we penetrate the unknown, the vaster and more marvelous it becomes.

—CHARLES A. LINDBERGH

~~~~~~

I consider the possibility that God was speaking to me through Gerard. We have been friends for forty-five years. In all that time, I have never considered Gerard saintly. But I have talked to him through many an emergency, counting on his long-sighted optimism. Broke? To Gerard it is simply a cash-flow situation. One that will soon be righted. Unlucky in love? To Gerard, "There are many other fish in the sea." Over the years I have come to depend on Gerard's optimistic perspective. And what is that optimism, really, but faith, however secular the terms in which it is couched?

85

Compared to Gerard, Jane is a recent addition to my life. Yet she shares with him the lamp of steady optimism. "You might enjoy your flight back home," she tells me now. I consider this unlikely, but not as out of the question as it seems. When I teach, I often call Jane for extra prayers that my teaching go well and smoothly—and it does. When I call to thank her, Jane is always nonchalant: of course her prayers are answered.

Now Jane dines on Dover sole. I order lamb chops. We eat for a while in amicable silence. I mull over Jane's suggestion that my flight home might be not merely bearable but actually enjoyable. "It would take a miracle," I catch myself thinking. Then I realize that for Jane, miracles are commonplace.

"What should I be praying for?" I ask Jane. "A smooth flight?"

"Oh, I think you can do better than that. Why not ask that you enjoy your flight, bumpy or smooth?"

The notion that I could enjoy a bumpy flight strikes me as radical. I say as much.

"You ride horses, don't you?" Jane asks.

"Yes, but what does that have to do with turbulence?"

"When your horse crow-hops, don't you enjoy it?"

I smile. Jane has me cornered. I do enjoy it when my horse acts up.

"Yes, I do enjoy it," I admit.

"So think of the plane like a spirited horse."

"I could try," I say dubiously.

"Of course you can," Jane wraps up the discussion.

For dessert, I order profiteroles, my favorite, at Jane's urging. I savor each bite. In between Jane's counsel and Gerard's, I might as well enjoy myself.

LATER THAT NIGHT, as I try for sleep, I catch myself worrying. I am in direct violation of Gerard's postponement strategy. I try to push worry aside. I slide from under the covers onto my knees. I pray:

Dear God,
Please help me to enjoy my flight,
bumpy or smooth. Please give me Jane's optimism.
Please let me think of the plane like a horse.
Amen.

Back under the covers, I find my worry lessened. I put the remainder of it off and fall asleep.

WINNING WINGS

While safely at your destination, it is common for anxiety to start building about the future return trip. Walking helps us stay in the moment by connecting us to our surroundings.

Take a twenty-minute solo walk in the place you are visiting. See if it doesn't restore a sense of optimism and maybe even inspire an insight or two.

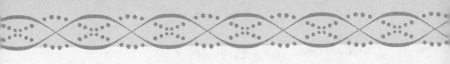

The Return

It is the day before my return flight. Today I have official permission to worry, but instead I think to myself, "I'll worry later." Gerard's postponement strategy has become second nature. I make a list of what I am packing to go home. The list is substantially the same as it was on the way out, but I have acquired two new books that I want to remember to take. I jot down the titles and begin to fill my suitcase. Tonight I am having dinner with Gerard, and so I leave out a change of clothes. I want to look elegant. At four p.m. I am still in my pajamas.

Glancing at the clock, I pray:

Dear God,
Please guide my packing.
Let me not forget anything.
Help me to dress well for Gerard.
Let me be elegant and practical.
Guide my hand in making up.
Amen.

~~~~~~

There isn't a flight goes by when I don't stare
out of the window and thank my stars for
what I'm seeing and feeling.

—RICHARD BRANSON, PILOT AND FOUNDER OF VIRGIN ATLANTIC

~~~~~~

Item by item, I pack. I remember to set aside the medicines I take at bedtime. At five o'clock I slip into the shower. After toweling myself dry, I dress in a tunic and slacks.

I am meeting Gerard at Pascalou. I plan on the smoked salmon. Making up carefully, I add an extra dab of mascara. I want to look my best.

To my relief, I catch a cab as soon as I step to the curb.

We nose into traffic, heading north to Pascalou. My driver is chatty. He brings up the weather (good) and the traffic (bad). Fighting congestion, we make our way block by block. We pull up at Pascalou fifteen minutes early. I pay off the cab and enter the restaurant. The maître d' fusses over me and shows me to a choice table. I order a bottle of sparkling water and settle in to wait for Gerard. He's quick to arrive, five minutes early. I kiss him hello.

~~~~~~

The man who flies an airplane . . .
must believe in the unseen.

—RICHARD BACH

~~~~~~

"You're looking spiffy," he compliments me.

"And you're looking debonair," I reply.

"So how are you doing?" Gerard asks. I know that he means "about flying."

"I've managed to postpone feeling terrified," I tell him. "I used your postponement technique."

"Very good," he replies.

"I'm afraid I've saved up all my terror for tonight," I confess.

Gerard clucks sympathetically.

"Maybe you can postpone it until tomorrow," he ventures.

"Maybe I can try," I venture.

"I'll bet you could," Gerard says thoughtfully. He turns the conversation to my teaching. I am always frightened before I teach. But in that arena, I have learned to postpone my anxiety. I have learned to look forward to the positive thrill of my students catching fire.

"So you need to look forward to the positives of flying," Gerard suggests. "Take your flight tomorrow. You'll be winging your way back home. And home is certainly something to look forward to."

Our entrées arrive, and we settle into eating. My fear of flying is successfully postponed as I focus on the

The Wright brothers flew through the
smoke screen of impossibility.

—DOROTHEA BRANDE

delicious salmon. After dessert—profiteroles again—it's time for me to get back to my lodgings. My flight is early in the morning. I have called a car service to pick me up at seven a.m. I don't want to risk not finding a cab.

"Good night, then. I'm glad we got a good visit in." Gerard kisses me good-bye. As luck would have it, a cab swerves to the curb. I clamber in.

Long flights give you more time to reflect, look around, experience your surroundings.

—MIKE FOALE, WHO HAS 374 DAYS LOGGED IN SPACE

Back at my hotel, I wait for fear to hit me, but it doesn't. Perhaps my subconscious is respecting the blockade that postpones my fear until the morning. I finish up my packing and settle into bed. I anticipate a sleepless night, but instead I drop off to sleep in minutes. My alarm is set for six.

I wake at five forty-five, before the buzzer sounds. I climb into my clothes and do my makeup. I am ready with a half hour to spare. I take out my journal and begin my daily three Morning Pages. I race through my prayers, writing out the names of my beloveds and, in my mind, bestowing blessings on each of them. I am on page two before it occurs to me that I am not frightened. I am many other things, among them impatient. I decide to go downstairs and wait for my car.

I do one last "idiot check" just in case I have forgotten something. I have not.

Down on street level, I discover my car service has arrived early. But what's this?

The hood is propped open and the driver is standing with jumper cables in hand. "Dead battery," he says to me. A cab pulls alongside. The cabbie pops his hood. My driver attaches the cables. It's five of seven. I don't want to risk the battery dying a second time.

"Thanks. I'll catch a cab," I tell my driver. He is dismayed, but I do not trust that the battery is fixed. I move off down the street, lugging my suitcase, and at the corner I raise my hand. I am worried there will be no cabs, but I spot a cab a block away, and it spots me. When it pulls up, the driver hops out to help with my suitcase. I tell him which airport and which carrier.

"Sure enough," he says. He noses the cab back into traffic. He drives assertively.

The ride to the airport is smooth and uneventful. I like my cabbie's driving. It feels speedy but safe.

~~~~~~

Be like the bird that, passing on her flight awhile on boughs too slight, feels them give way beneath her, and yet sings, knowing that she hath wings.

—VICTOR HUGO

~~~~~~

When we pull up at curbside check-in, I am relieved. I have plenty of time. I tip the cabbie extravagantly. He is surprised and grateful. I tell the skycap my flight number, destination, and time of departure.

"You're early," he says.

"Yes, I know. It's on purpose," I reply, handing over my passport.

WINNING WINGS

We all have the ability to postpone worry. It is simply a matter of deciding to do it. When worry rears its head, tell yourself, "I'll think about it later," and turn your thoughts to the present. This is a technique we can develop, like strengthening a muscle. The more times we do it, the easier it gets.

[Flying] fosters fantasies of childhood, of omnipotence, rapid shifts of being, miraculous moments; it stirs our capacity for dreaming.

—JOYCE CAROL OATES

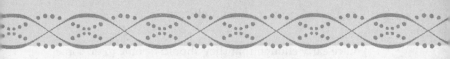

Companionship

You!" I hear a voice behind me. I spin around and encounter my middle-seat neighbor from my last flight.

"You!" I echo. "I'm headed back."

"Me, too. We shouldn't be so shocked. After all, there are only so many flights."

"Still, it's nice."

"What's your seat number? Maybe we can sit together."

I stand to one side while my neighbor checks in. "Can we sit together?" I ask the ticket agent.

"You'll have to change your seats at the gate, but

you're early enough that they should be able to do something for you."

"Thanks. That would be great."

Boarding passes in hand, we head for security. This time I have remembered to pack my pendant. Doffing my belt, shoes, and sweater, I expect to pass the checkpoint without incident. But no. I am called to a bench and my bottle of contact lens solution violates the rules. It is only after relinquishing the bottle that I am allowed through. In the meanwhile, my traveling companion has also been stopped. The offense? Wearing a medical alert bracelet.

"These things are supposed to make life easier and safer!"

"Just not here."

"Let's get to the gate and see about our seats," I suggest.

I pray:

Thank you, God, for contriving to give me company.
Help me not to "catch" any fear.
Help us to get adjoining seats.
Amen.

At the gate, there is only one woman behind the desk. We explain that we are friends and that we want to travel together, if possible. She punches in our request.

I owned the world that hour as I rode over it . . . free of the earth, free of the mountains, free of the clouds, but how inseparably I was bound to them.

—CHARLES A. LINDBERGH

"I can give you an aisle and a window in row twenty-three—will that do?"

We confer. It's awfully far back. Both of us would be giving up our "better" seats to sit together. We decide it's worth it and tell the agent to go ahead and make us new boarding passes. She punches a few buttons. Her computer whirs and—voilà! New seat assignments. We have an hour left before boarding.

"Off to the newsstand?" my neighbor ventures. "It's time for tabloids."

WINNING WINGS

Experience with flying will teach us where we like to sit. For some of us, it's the window seat. For others, the middle or aisle. Arriving early at our departure gate gives us the chance to request a seat in our comfort zone.

The very existence of aviation is proof that man, given the will, has the capacity to accomplish deeds that seem impossible.

—EDDIE RICKENBACKER

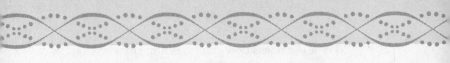

Treat Yourself

I'll get the tabloids," my neighbor unexpectedly volunteers.

"I'll get the snacks," I offer.

Between the two of us, we spend thirty-four dollars.

Making our way back to the gate, we find two seats in the waiting area. My neighbor snags a tabloid. The cover headline asserts that a popular movie star is secretly gay.

"I don't care if he is," I say.

"It's the cover-up that's the issue."

"Some cover-up. Twenty-year marriage and three children."

"How could she not know?"

"Maybe she does know and loves him anyway. Maybe he's a genuine bisexual."

"You're awfully calm," my neighbor observes.

"I'm putting off my terror," I respond. I explain Gerard's postponement strategy.

"It really works?"

"It has so far."

"Better than prayers?"

"Who knows? I use the two together, like:"

Dear God,
Please postpone my fears
and P.S. keep the plane aloft.
Amen.

I laugh, and my neighbor joins me. Gerard's postponement strategy is working.

Now our pilot and copilot step up to the gate. The agent buzzes them through. Neither one of them is flushed. They both look competent and well rested. I pray:

Thank you, God, for giving us a good pilot and copilot.
Thank you for their sobriety and expertise.
Please help us to have faith in their skills.

A flock of flight attendants arrives at our gate. They look trim and athletic. I pray again:

Thank you, God, for giving us a good crew.
Thank you for making them crisp and alert.
Thank you for my trust in them.
Amen.

Our gate is now filled to capacity. I scan the crowd and find myself feeling a spirit of camaraderie. My paranoia about terrorists has vanished.

"Good-looking bunch, eh?" I comment to my neighbor.

"No terrorists?"

"No. I don't think so." I laugh.

"You're quite the optimist today," my neighbor ventures.

"I might as well believe the best," I state.

"I guess." My neighbor sounds doubtful.

"Faith is contagious," I assert. "I caught mine from my friends Jane and Gerard. Jane has forty-plus years on a spiritual path. Gerard just has optimistic DNA."

"You're lucky to have spiritual friends. My friends scoffed when I tried telling them about prayer."

"They say the only ones who scoff at prayer are those who haven't tried it enough."

"I wish I'd said that to them."

"No point in getting in a pissing match."

"No. I suppose not."

WINNING WINGS

Once you are at the airport, you are in a period of waiting—your own "holding pattern"—as the many elements are prepared for your flight. Waiting in lines, waiting at the gate, waiting to board, waiting to be seated, waiting to take off. You are at the mercy of others for the time being. What better time to treat yourself to a little frivolous luxury? It's okay to be a bit naughty in what you choose.

For example:

Treat yourself to a magazine or book that you would "never otherwise buy."

Treat yourself to a decadent snack or beverage.

Buy yourself some cozy socks or a neck pillow.

The idea is to take care of yourself, to spoil yourself a little. See if you don't feel a little bit calmer and better cared for as you move through the various stages and phases of your travel day.

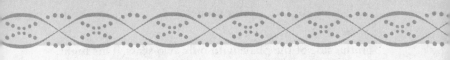

Make Believe
You're Brave

Once again, we are boarding the plane by blocks. After the first class and premier travelers, our block is called next.

"Here we go!" I exclaim.

"You're so cheerful!"

"I'm practicing my Rodgers and Hammerstein— 'Make believe you're brave and the trick will take you far. You may be as brave as you make believe you are.'"

"I love that song. Maybe I should try it."

"I think it works."

"You're full of things that work."

We make our way down the crowded aisle to our seats. We are flying a small, "regional" jet. We're seated on the side of the plane with only two seats. This flight, we will have no eavesdroppers.

"Can you say a prayer?" my neighbor asks.

"Of course." And so I pray:

Dear God,
Let us fly safely.
Guide our pilot and our crew.
Put your protective strength
beneath our wings.
Let us take off, fly, and land safely.
Thank you for your help.
Amen.

"You pray much better than I do. I'm not specific."

"Being specific reassures me. I find it grounding"

"It's starting to rain," my neighbor muses, glancing toward the window.

Sure enough, the plane's windows are spattered, then streaked.

"We can still take off. It's landing that's tricky in a storm."

The plane backs from the gate and taxis down a long

runway. At the end, it turns and stops, revving its engines. Then it noses into the storm.

~~~~~~

If the heavens be penetrable, and no lets, it were not amiss to make wings and fly up, and some new-fangled wits should some time or other find out.

—ROBERT BURTON

~~~~~~

"Here we go," I say as the plane lifts off. We bank sharply, and my neighbor clutches my arm. "It's okay," I say, although my own heart is hammering. Outside the window, I see buildings at askew angles. "It's okay," I repeat. "We're just turning." My neighbor releases my arm. We took off to the northeast, and our destination lies to the southwest. The steep turn is necessary. The plane levels off and heads in the right direction. There is a grinding noise as the landing gear retracts.

"We're on our way!" I exclaim. "We'll leave the storm behind us."

"From your mouth to God's ear," says my neighbor.

The pilot's reassuring voice comes on the air: "Ladies and gentlemen, please keep your seat belts securely fastened until we reach our cruising altitude of thirty-two thousand feet. We may experience some turbulence, but it is nothing to be alarmed about."

"That's easy for him to say!" exclaims my neighbor. There is a bump and then a sickening drop. I pray:

Dear God,
Please guide us to smooth air.
Amen.

The plane climbs again. Again there is a bump and then a drop. It feels like the stomach-churning drop on a roller coaster.

God, help us!
Amen.

My neighbor prays, clutching again at my arm.

"We'll be out of this soon," I say soothingly. The plane shimmies. I pray:

Dear God,
Please, please, give us smooth air.
Guide our pilot. End this turbulence.
Amen.

"Do you think God is listening?" my neighbor asks.

"God is always listening," I answer, telling my neighbor what I am telling myself.

The plane bucks more violently. I look toward the cockpit, to the chair where the flight attendant sits facing us. The flight attendant looks a little worried—or is that my imagination? The plane bucks again.

"I'm scared," says my neighbor. "Aren't you?"

"We're going to be fine," I say. Again I tell my neighbor what I am telling myself. "Do you want to pray?" I ask.

"Yes!"

"Give me your hand."

I take my neighbor's hand and I pray aloud:

Dear God,
This turbulence is frightening.
We are trying to trust you and our pilot.
Let us feel your reassurance.

Guide us to smooth air.
Help us to be calm.
Help us to have faith.
Thank you.
Amen.

My neighbor continues to hold my hand. The plane shimmies again. I find myself clutching tightly to my neighbor's hand. I pray:

Please, God, end this turbulence.

The plane surges upward into smooth air. An answered prayer!

WINNING WINGS

"Make believe you're brave, and the trick will take you far" is another way of wording a common philosophy. "Just do it," "Feel the fear and do it anyway," and "Act as if" are other catchphrases referring to the same idea. Regardless of how *we feel*, we can *act* correctly. "Act *as if* you have confidence," wise mentors often advise. And when the advisee does just that, his or her confidence seems to build.

Try acting *as if* in one instance on your flight. For example:

Smile at your seatmate. Maybe he or she will become a new friend.

Thank your pilot *before* the flight begins, as you are boarding, instead of only when you deplane.

Allow yourself to display a positive attitude. Act *as if* you are completely at home on the plane. See if it adjusts how you feel, if the trick does indeed "take you far."

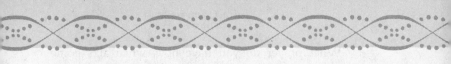

Loving Kindness

Thank you," says my neighbor, retrieving the tell-tale palm. "Your prayers calm me down. I think it's great good luck that we are on the same flight." She pauses, then interjects, "But we forgot to say thank you."

"Go ahead!"

Thank you, God, for answering our prayers.
Thank you for ending the turbulence.
Thank your for smooth air.
Amen.

"You see? That was a perfect prayer!"

"What prayer do you have now, when all's going well?"

I pray:

Thank you, God, for the smooth sailing.
Thank you for the calm.
Please let us feel your presence.
Let us trust your loving kindness.
Amen.

"You do trust God's loving kindness," my neighbor declares.

"Do I? I guess I do."

"You expect miracles."

"I expect help," I admit.

"I think it's a miracle we're on the same flight," my neighbor ventures.

"I wouldn't call it a miracle, but I think it's very nice."

"What you don't know is that for me it's an answered prayer. I asked God to give me a seatmate as nice as you—and then I got you!"

"I'm flattered," I demur.

"You can't really know the difference it made. I

went from flying in stark terror to flying with mere apprehension."

"I'd like to see us both fly fearlessly," I assert. "Jane and Gerard both think that's possible."

"What does Jane do?" my neighbor asks.

"She's an actress."

"Well, no wonder she can fly fearlessly. She's used to pretending."

"That hadn't occurred to me."

"And Gerard?"

"He's a teacher."

"Another one! He has to pretend to be calm in front of the little ones."

"So now that you've discounted both Jane and Gerard, do you feel better?"

"No. But I feel familiar. Scared."

"I am going to trust Jane and Gerard. That makes me feel much better, and better is what I am trying to feel."

"Look at the sunset, then."

I look past my seatmate out the window. The sun is setting in Technicolor. The sky is apricot. A ribbon of cerise lies along the horizon.

"It's beautiful," I exclaim.

"Beautiful enough to make a person believe in God?" my neighbor pushes.

"I wouldn't have thought of it that way, but yes," I answer.

"Ever since I met you, I've been trying to believe in God," confesses my neighbor.

"Fake it till you make it," I jibe.

"Meaning?"

"Pretend you believe in God and you will find that you do."

"Did you have to fake it?" my neighbor pries.

"I prayed every morning and every night. At first I was praying to nothing. And then I started praying to something. Eventually, I called that something 'God,'" I answer.

"So now you're a believer?" my neighbor asks bluntly.

"Yes," I admit. "Now I pray about anything and everything. For example, 'Thank you, God, for the glorious sunset.'"

"Thank you, God, for the beautiful distraction?" my neighbor jokes.

"Exactly."

Two and a half hours pass uneventfully, and I find

myself becoming absorbed in my reading. As the announcement comes on letting us know we are approaching our destination, I realize that the flight has, indeed, been peaceful—even enjoyable. I breathe a sigh of gratitude.

Outside the window we fly over freight hangars. Trucks appear toy size, then larger. We pass the lights at the runway's end. We fly lower, then lower, finally touching ground with a satisfying *thunk*. I realize I do not have my neighbor's name. I ask for it. My neighbor responds with name and e-mail. I hand over the same.

"I will be flying again in three weeks, when my daughter's baby is due," I announce.

"I'll pray for you to have an unfrightened flight," replies my neighbor.

"And you. Do you need to fly again soon?" I ask.

"No. Not that I know of," my neighbor replies.

"When you do fly, you'll remember our tricks?" I nag gently.

"Prayer and tabloids, but I don't think of prayer as a trick," my neighbor answers.

"No, probably not. You'll remember it, though?" I badger.

"Yes." My neighbor's answer is firm.

"It has really been a pleasure, traveling with you," I conclude.

"Ditto." The plane pulls to a stop at the gate. There is the *ping* that tells us we can release our seat belts. My neighbor has a suitcase in the overhead bin. So do I. I will pick up the other at baggage claim .

"So it's good-bye," I say.

"Good-bye for now." And with that, my neighbor disappears into the swirling crowd.

~~~~~~

I fly because it releases my mind from the
tyranny of petty things.

—ANTOINE DE SAINT-EXUPÉRY

~~~~~~

I retrieve my bag and make my way to the shuttle. We head north through the desert landscape. An hour later, the shuttle pulls into my stop. A taxi is waiting to take me up the mountain to home.

WINNING WINGS

A swift way to put ourselves in touch with a benevolent Something is to make a list of things we love. As quickly as you can, list ten things you love. For example:

I love raspberries.

I love blue jays.

I love Robert's photography.

I love . . .

I love . . .

Listing your loves instills a belief in a benevolent universe.

Home

Home: an adobe house nestled amid the piñon trees. My writing room juts out from the body of the house. It is ringed by birdfeeders, and the traffic flow keeps me entertained. I have three weeks before I am due to fly again, and so I settle into my daily routine of morning writing, break for lunch, afternoon writing, break for dinner, evening writing if I desire. My friends tell me I look nervous. I am nervous. I am waiting for the phone call that tells me Domenica has gone into labor. Then I am to race to the airport and catch the first available flight into Chicago.

As the days tick past and the phone call doesn't come, I find myself reluctant to leave the house for fear of missing the call. My daughter's husband, Tony, has promised me that he will call both my landline and my cell phone until he reaches me. His assurances help, but do not entirely quell, my anxieties. It is my daughter's first pregnancy, and it hasn't been an easy one. My prayer now is that her delivery goes smoothly. The baby's due date is July 4. How wonderful to have fireworks on your birthday!

"First babies traditionally come late," I am counseled. One woman tells me that she went to her daughter's on the due date only to have the baby take ten more days to arrive. "It was the worst ten days of my life," she tells me. And so, difficult as it is, I stay put in my own house, although my consciousness is brooding over my daughter's nest in the Windy City.

"How are you doing?" I call daily to ask. My daughter is not a whiner, but she does tell me, "I have difficulty sleeping. The baby takes my lying down as a cue to swim around." I remember my own pregnancy and the great discomfort I had at the end—and my daughter is much smaller than I am. How much more uncomfortable she must be.

"Just keep trying to sleep," I urge her, knowing that

fatigue makes everything worse. "She's just so little," I tell my friends.

"Lots of five-foot-tall women have had lots of babies," they strive to reassure me. In my morning prayers, I now include a request for Domenica to have a safe and smooth delivery. What with the baby's swimming motions, I wonder if the birth will come early. I stick close to the phone, calling my daughter once a day, then twice a day—not wanting to nag, yet wanting to be supportive.

"I look like I'm about to pop," my daughter remarks. She and her husband take birthing classes, but she still wonders what to expect.

"Labor pains are misnamed," I tell her. "What you will feel is a band of muscles tightening, like a giant rubber band."

"Thank you, Mommy," Domenica says. I ask her if she wants me to come to town early, but she says no. She wants only her husband present in the delivery room. And so I resign myself to more waiting, leaping to the phone every time it rings.

WINNING WINGS

"Home is where the heart is," they say, and it welcomes us with its familiar arms after our trip. As you enter your home, look around. Notice what you appreciate about it and notice one thing you might be willing and able to do to improve it. Taking care of our homes, we take care of ourselves. Once you have allowed yourself a gentle rest, light a candle or a stick of incense—something that indicates your home is a sacred space.

All agreed that the sensation of coasting
on the air was delightful.
—OCTAVE CHANUTE

Taking Flight

Finally the call comes, mid-afternoon on July 3. Domenica has gone into labor. Nerves aflutter, I call for a ticket and get a seat on an early-morning flight the next day, the fourth. There is plenty to do until then.

Tiger Lily needs to go back to the boarding kennel, to the place I now laughingly call "the spa." I pack her special food and her medicines—she takes heart medicine and follows a low-calorie, high-priced food regime—then I snap a leash to her collar and herd her out to the car. I settle her on the backseat, where her soft and fluffy sheepskin throw awaits.

"You'll be a good girl, won't you?" I ask. She doesn't need the lecture. She seems to enjoy the spa. (Although she does some ego-gratifying spins and pirouettes—"Hi, Mommy!"—when I come to pick her up.) The drive to the spa is short. I've phoned ahead to make sure they can take her.

"Tiiiiiger Lilee!" croons the woman behind the desk when we come in the door.

She opens a gate and shepherds Tiger Lily into her domain. Tiger Lily trots off eagerly to meet her playmates.

"Good-bye, girl," I croon across the gate to Tiger Lily's disappearing tail. An inner door opens, and she is set free to play with a pack of playmates. The door swings shut, and she is out of sight.

"When will you be picking her up?" the woman at the desk asks me. I have not filled in all the paperwork.

"I don't know when I will be back. I'll call you. My daughter is having her first baby. She's in labor right now, actually."

"Congratulations, Grandma!"

Grandma . . . Granny . . . Am I ready to be a granny? My own granny was called "Mimi." I like that better. Nana. Grandma. None of them sounds good to me. I think I will want to be called whatever the baby can say.

Driving home, I recite my possible names: Granny, Grandma, Nana, Mimi, Grandmother . . .

Once home, I pack my suitcase. I figure I will be staying about ten days. Once again I use a list so as not to forget anything. I begin with my passport and proceed through clothing and sundries. I pack my medicine separately. At eleven o'clock, bedtime, I realize that I am not afraid. I am flying in the morning, and I feel calm. This strikes me as miraculous. I pray:

Thank you, God, for my calm.
Thank you for my lack of fear.
Please help me to sleep.
Let me wake early and forget nothing.
Let my morning ride come on time.
Get me to the shuttle with time to spare.
Get the shuttle to the airport on time.
Let my flight be uneventful.
Thank you for your help.
Amen.

Mercifully, I drop straight off to sleep. I sleep through the night, waking at six, before my alarm. I make myself a pot of strong coffee and take myself to the page. I record my mood: excited yet tranquil. I'm not frightened of the impending flight. I am frightened for my daughter. I phone her husband at the hospital and learn that she is still in labor. They have given her a strong drug to induce accelerated labor, but no luck so far. "Give her my love," I tell Tony. "I'm on my way to the airport."

I eat chopped pineapple for breakfast. My friend, the novelist John Bowers, is set to drive me to the shuttle. At ten of eight, he pulls in my driveway. He's ten minutes early, but I am ready.

"All set?" he asks. "Can I carry your suitcase?"

"Yes and yes," I answer.

"I set two alarms," he tells me. "I didn't want to take any chances." Clearly, John's nerves are a match for my own. "I like to get to the airport early," he adds.

Piloting his way down the mountain, John keeps up a steady stream of conversation. I am too excited to focus on what he is telling me. We reach the shuttle stop at Water and Sandoval Streets with twenty minutes to spare. John parks carefully, leaving space at the curb for the shuttle van.

"Are they usually on time?" he asks.

"Yes," I assure him. I am trying to reassure myself.

In addition to being a novelist, John is a first-rate, world-class medievalist. He is set to deliver a paper on Chaucer as seen by Tolkien. He's excited by the prospect and fills our waiting minutes with an overview. Listening to John, I check in with myself: still not scared. Right on time, the shuttle pulls to the curb.

"Thank you, John," I breathe.

"Let me get your suitcase," he offers.

~~~~~~

> Birds in flight, claims the architect Vincenzo
> Volentieri, are not between places—they carry their
> places with them. We never wonder where they live:
> they are at home in the sky, in flight. Flight is
> their way of being in the world.
>
> —GEOFF DYER

~~~~~~

Mike, the shuttle driver, name on shirt, checks off my name from his list of prospective passengers. "You're on American?" he asks, glancing at his notes.

"Yes," I confirm. "Can I sit up front by you?"

"Yes. Let me help you on."

"You're all set?" John asks.

"Yes, I am. Thank you for the ride."

Mike pulls a small stool from the van. He sets it at an angle for me to climb aboard. I swing up into the shotgun seat. Nervously, I fasten my seat belt. More passengers arrive, and Mike checks them off his list. He stops at nine. All that is expected. He locks the baggage compartment and then swings up onto the driver's seat. He speaks into an intercom: "Base, this is Mike. I've got nine." He pulls away from the curb.

For fifteen minutes he navigates the maze of Santa Fe streets. Then he is in the clear and taking the ramp for the interstate toward Albuquerque. For another ten minutes we are passing through the outskirts of Santa Fe. Then houses give way to desert and we have forty miles of desolate terrain. *How is my daughter?* I wonder. She has been in labor for twenty hours. I keep my eyes peeled for the Indian ponies, but I don't spot any. Instead there are a few head of cattle nibbling the sparse vegetation.

"Are we on time?" I ask Mike. My nerves are ajar.

"Yes," he replies. "We should just miss the Albuquerque rush hour."

Roadside signs tick off the number of miles remaining. At fourteen miles, I try to relax. We take the exit for the Albuquerque International Sunport and follow the signs for departures. American is the first stop. Mike pulls to the curb, swings down, and opens the baggage compartment.

"It's the black one with the red ribbon," I volunteer. He wrestles my bag to the curb.

"Thank you so much," I say, handing him a tip. I tug my bag to the curbside check-in. The clock on the wall tells me I have two hours until takeoff, an hour and a half until boarding. I hand over my passport and credit card. I'm checking one bag. I tell the ticket agent my flight and destination. He, as usual, tells me I am early. I reply that I know that and I prefer that. He gives a little shrug indicating that I am crazy. I thank him and head into the terminal.

I make my way to security, surrendering my passport. After a minute's deliberation, the security agent scrawls "OK" on my boarding pass and waves me on through. Now the familiar drill: off with my jacket, my shoes, my belt, and my pendant. Farewell to my purse and briefcase. No, I have no computer. Can I stand in the footprints and raise my hands above my head? (I can.)

"Go on. You're finished," I am told. The attendant sounds irritated, but it could just be my nerves.

I set about retrieving my belongings and sit on a bench to put on my shoes.

Thank you, God, for getting me past security.
Amen.

I remember to put on my pendant. I fasten my belt, slip back into my jacket. I gather up my purse and brief-case. Now I am off to the newsstand, where I will purchase tabloids. I select five and try to ignore the clerk's comment, "I guess you've got plenty."

After purchasing my reading material I go to the coffee stand, where I get a large iced coffee with half-and-half. It costs six dollars. I head on toward my gate. I take a seat and open a tabloid. I sink into reading. I am absorbed for an hour. Then I look to the gate and see that the scroll announces another city, not Chicago. I go to the desk and ask if there has been a gate change. Yes, there has. Gathering up my belongings, I hurry to the new gate. "Chicago," reads the scroll. Nonetheless, I check in with the attendant at the gate. Yes, I am in the right place.

The attendant announces we will be boarding by zones. I am zone three. I fold up my tabloid and put it with my other magazines. I wait out the ten minutes until they get to my zone. Once again, we are flying on a smaller, "regional" jet. Storage space is at a premium. I place my briefcase in an overhead bin, stowing my magazines at my feet under the seat in front of me. I wedge my purse there, too.

An announcement comes over the air. It is raining in Chicago. We will be delayed a half hour in taking off. I fight a wave of annoyance. I resent the delay. I resent every minute that stands between me and my daughter. Surely she must have given birth by now. She has been in labor nearly a full day. I pray:

Please help her, God.
Please give her stamina.

I turn back to my tabloid. I have read the headline stories. Now I am in the back of the tabloid, where they advertise weight-loss herbs and potions. There are before and after photos of women in bikinis. Under each picture is the amount of weight lost: twenty pounds, thirty pounds, forty pounds. One woman lost an astonishing sixty pounds. I contemplate sending off for the supplement.

Ping. We are asked to turn off our cell phones

and fasten our seat belts. The tabloid has done its job, and a half hour has passed. Our jet taxis toward the runway.

At runway's end, we turn and the engines rev higher. With a little lurch, we begin speeding down the runway for takeoff. *Faster,* I will the jet. *Faster.* I pray:

Dear God, please let us take off safely.
Please help us gain altitude smoothly.
May our flight be swift and without incident.
Amen.

I notice that my prayer lacks fear. I actually feel confident that all will go well. I will soon be reunited with my daughter. "Oh, my God," I think to myself. "I may have actually gotten over my fear of flying!" The jet banks sharply to the left. I am not frightened. Outside the window, buildings appear in miniature. "We're just getting on course," I tell myself. "We're just making a turn." The plane rights itself. We're headed to Chicago.

Ping. The seat belt sign flicks off. The pilot speaks: "Ladies and gentlemen, you are now at liberty to move about the cabin, although we ask that when you are seated you keep your seat belt firmly fastened, as we may yet encounter unexpected turbulence."

The prospect of further unexpected turbulence doesn't frighten me. I reach for a magazine and am soon engrossed in the details of a celebrity wedding. Above all else, the wedding sounds fun. The happy couple rented tents for a hundred of their friends to camp out over the wedding weekend. Food was down-home barbeque. There was an open bar.

All in all, it sounds very festive.

I finish my reading and reach for another magazine. This one, too, features a Hollywood wedding, but its emphasis is on sour grapes, not on who came and had a wonderful time, but on who wasn't invited—the bride's family. "Wedding Snub," the story is dubbed. I skim the bad news and then decide to stretch my legs. I make it all the way down the aisle before the plane begins to bump and buck. *Ping.* The seat-belt sign illuminates. I make my way unsteadily back to my seat. This is the unexpected turbulence the pilot warned us about. I fasten my seat belt, alert but not anxious. Surely by now my daughter must be a mother. I pray for her comfort. I pray for my own:

Dear God,
Please help our pilot
to find us smooth air.
Please help us ride out this turbulence.
Thank you for your help.
Amen.

I notice that while I am praying, my prayers are without panic. I feel I am petitioning God but that God is already on the case. My friend Jane told me that I always have a choice between faith and fear. I seem to be opting for faith. My friend Gerard told me I could always postpone fear. I seem to be doing exactly that.

There is one prayer I feel with my whole heart:

Dear God,
Thank you for healing my fear.
Thank you for giving me confidence
in your loving confidence.
Allow me to enjoy this journey.
Allow me to enjoy future journeys.
Please accept my gratitude.
My heart brims over.
Amen.

A short while later, the pilot comes on the air one more time: "Ladies and gentlemen, please keep your seat belts securely fastened. We are beginning our final descent. We should be at the gate in twenty more minutes. That's fifteen minutes ahead of schedule." Five minutes pass, and then the landing gear grinds into place. I find the sound reassuring. It signals to me that our flight is nearly safely over.

~~~~~~

> For my part I know nothing with any certainty
> but the sight of the stars makes me dream.
>
> —VINCENT VAN GOGH

~~~~~~

With ten minutes until touchdown, I reach for my last magazine. It contains an article with color photos of celebrity pilots. There's Harrison Ford; both Angelina Jolie and Brad Pitt. Most noticeably, there is John Travolta, who owns his own jumbo jet. The photos feature the celebrities planeside and in the cockpit. They are smiling heartfelt smiles. They love to fly. I pray:

Dear God,
Bless these amateur pilots.
Give them skill and expertise.
Help them to fly safely.
Help them to be without fear.
Grant them protection.
Put your wings beneath their wings.
Amen.

Our jet descends smoothly with not a trace of turbulence. We streak past some runway lights, then we touch ground. It is a textbook landing. The pilot fires the jets in reverse, slowing the plane to a safe speed for taxiing to the gate. I pray:

We made it, God!

And I pray:

Thank you! Hosannah in the highest!

I gather my magazines, briefcase, and purse. I wait for the announcement that we are free to use our cell phones. When it comes, I dial my daughter, expecting to get her husband. Instead, Domenica herself answers. "Sweet-heart!" I say when I hear her voice. "Are you okay?"

"You have a beautiful granddaughter, Serafina. She's lovely. And I'm fine. How was your flight?"

"My flight was good."

"Not too scary?"

"I was fine."

"That's terrific, Mom!"

"I think so. I'll see you in less than an hour."

"Great."

I hang up the phone and focus on the business at hand. I have my suitcase to retrieve and a taxi to catch. I will go directly to the hospital.

At baggage claim, I look for my bag with its gay, telltale ribbon. It's easy to spot and easy to heft. I have packed lightly. I make my way to the taxi line. I feel like shouting, "Let me go first. My daughter just had a baby!" But the line is not too long, and so I impatiently wait my turn. My cabbie has a shaved head and tattoos twining up the back of his neck. I give him the name and address of the hospital. We set out. Traffic is heavy, and my cabbie is talkative.

"Good flight?" he inquires.

"Very good."

"No bumps?"

"A few," I respond.

"Then I'm surprised you'd say the flight was good."

"We had turbulence on takeoff and then a little bit later on. No big deal."

"So you're not a frightened flyer." My cabbie glances at me in the rearview mirror.

"I am. Or I was. This flight I felt calm," I hear myself say with some surprise.

"You'd be surprised how many frightened flyers I get."

"Do you take a survey?" I ask.

"I ask. Gives us something to talk about, you know." My cabbie chuckles. "You say you used to be afraid."

"Yes. I used to be terrified."

"You're safer in an airplane than you are in this cab."

"I've been told that. It didn't really make any difference in how I felt."

"No. Fear isn't logical."

"That's what I always said!"

"But this time you weren't frightened. What made the difference?"

"My daughter was in labor. I was focused on her, not

me. I have a friend who told me to just postpone my fear and keep on postponing it."

"That's a good one. I haven't heard it before."

"One way or another, this time I was not afraid. And I prayed."

"If you don't mind, I'll borrow your techniques. You've got no idea how many people who ride with me are afraid of flying. If I had to guess, I'd say one out of three or four."

"I think what makes us afraid is that when we fly, we are out of control. We place our life in the hands of our pilot, someone who's usually a complete stranger. And then there's the claustrophobia factor. It's worse on a small jet like the one I just flew. That doesn't help. Of course, turbulence makes it worse for most people. And so I pray."

"I pray when traffic is bad."

"Yes. When the chips are down we finally turn to God. Thankfully, God is a good sport."

"What do you mean by that?"

"I mean that God answers our prayers instead of saying, 'What took you so long!'"

At this thought my cabbie laughs. Traffic is thick, but

we are enjoying the conversation. I am struck by the cabbie's estimate of the number of fearful people flying. It's far more than I would have imagined. It occurs to me that with such a high percentage of frightened flyers, the airlines would somehow acknowledge the problem. A simple speech would help. Something along the lines of, "We know that many of you are frightened to fly. We want to assure you of your safety. Your pilot and crew are skilled. Even in the event of turbulence, we know exactly what to do. Trust our expertise. Sit back and enjoy the flight. Bon voyage."

I tell my cabbie my idea about a speech. He laughs and says, "You didn't put anything in about God."

"'Let us all pray for a safe flight.' How's that?" I ask.

"I think it might frighten people," my cabbie says after a moment. "After all, God is a last resort."

"I suppose that's true," I muse. "On my last flight, I sat next to someone who asked if I was praying. I figured what the hell and said yes. After my confession, we prayed together. It calmed us both down."

My cabbie laughs again. He says, "Maybe you could try praying about this traffic!"

The traffic is so thick it is nearly at a standstill. I think, "What could a prayer hurt?" I pray:

Dear God,
Please give us a hand.
Please thin this traffic.
Please let us make this trip more quickly.
Please give us safety and speed.
Amen.

"That's a good prayer, all right," my cabbie announces. "I think I'll try it myself. Look! The traffic is thinning out! I can speed up a little."

"That's great. My daughter just had a baby and I'm eager to get to the hospital."

"First grandchild?"

"Yes."

"I'll have you there in twenty minutes."

And so I settle back, watching the Chicago skyline draw ever closer. The hospital is near the flank of the John Hancock building. I keep my eyes fixed on that landmark. My cabbie pilots his way closer. Fifteen minutes elapse. True to his word, we are on the side streets near the Hancock. In twenty minutes, we are at the hospital. Forty dollars plus tip.

I step up to the reception desk. I give my daughter's married name and I am issued a visitor's pass. She is on the eleventh floor. The elevator is swift and modern. The entire hospital is modern. I follow the signs directing me to room 1103. Stepping inside, I am overcome with emotion. My daughter lies in bed, cradling her newborn in her arms. She looks radiant.

"Mom! Meet Serafina!" she exclaims.

"Hello, Serafina! Hello, Domenica!" I step bedside to kiss my daughter. Her husband hovers protectively. "Hello, Tony!" I greet him.

"Beautiful, isn't she?" he responds.

"Domenica, Serafina, or both?"

"Both." He laughs.

The door to the room swings open and Domenica's father steps into the room. He is followed by his wife and two other daughters—a full entourage.

"Dad!" Domenica exclaims. "Dad, Serafina. Serafina, Grandfather."

Everyone laughs appreciatively.

"Would you like to hold her?" Domenica asks her father. She carefully transfers the baby to his arms.

"She's the size you were," he tells his preteen daughter. She peers at the baby more closely. Tony offers a chair to the new grandfather. He takes it gratefully and sits with care. Cradling Serafina, his face softens. Clearly,

he loves the child already. For the next forty-five minutes, he rocks and cradles her. At six pounds three
ounces, Serafina is a small baby, but a healthy one.

"I'll take her," Domenica says when the baby starts to
fuss. She offers Serafina a breast, and the baby latches on
eagerly. "There you go," Domenica croons.

The conversation in the room turns general. "How
was your flight?" Domenica's father asks me.

"Pretty good. Just a little turbulence," I answer.

"Same with ours. I hate turbulence. Don't you?"

"This time it didn't bother me," I reply. "I prayed for
a safe flight."

"Maybe I should try that."

"And I had a trick from my friend Gerard—postpone
your fear and keep on postponing it."

"That's a good one!" Domenica's father exclaims. "I
could try that, too."

"My final trick is to buy tabloids," I confess. "There's

The bluebird carries the sky on his back.

—HENRY DAVID THOREAU

something very calming about other people's disasters. Celebrity catastrophes particularly cheer me up."

"I can see that."

"Mom. Dad. You'll both need to get over your fear of flying if you're going to come visit us."

"I'll feel the fear and visit you anyway," says her father.

"I wasn't afraid this time," I volunteer. "Maybe I'm cured."

"Maybe it's because you were flying for a good cause—Serafina." Domenica gently chucks her baby under the chin. "*Shhh!* She's sleeping!"

Serafina's sleep is the signal for an exodus. Her grandfather and his crew tiptoe from the room. Tony's parents tiptoe in. They bend over and peer at the tiny bundle.

"She's sleeping," Domenica whispers.

"She's beautiful," I whisper to the new arrivals.

"Yes!" they whisper back.

For the better part of an hour, we stay whispering. Domenica looks radiant cradling her daughter. Tony stands at bedside, a proud sentinel. No one wants to break the trance. Finally, Tony's mother whispers to me. "Dinner?" I realize I haven't eaten all day. "Yes. Dinner." I nod.

I will soon learn that Tony's parents are deeply hospitable. Dinner is at a fine restaurant, where they insist on picking up the tab. I will be staying with them for the next few days. I find their household immaculate. Domenica has furnished them with a grocery list for me, and their larder is stocked with my favorites. I have fresh chopped pineapple for a bedtime snack. Yogurt and berries are my breakfast. I feel thoroughly spoiled.

Day two at the hospital finds Domenica mastering the subtleties of breast-feeding. Serafina has a series of cues—tiny sounds and mouth movements that translate: "Feed me now" or "Not just yet." Domenica is alert to the cues, although both she and Tony look tired. His parents, "the Frenzel grandparents," continue their thoughtfulness, bringing Tony his favorite sandwich from a posh deli. They take a grocery list for Tony and Domenica's home refrigerator.

Day three finds the new little family trekking from the hospital to home. They've taken lessons on proper car-seat protocol, and the trip is made without incident. The Frenzels and I help them settle in. Dinner is carry-out from a favorite restaurant, Sai Cafe.

"Thank you, thank you," Domenica murmurs. She is grateful for any and all help. We don't want to overstay our welcome, but we do want to be a support. I plan to transfer households from the Frenzels' to judge Michele Lawrence's. Michele is a longtime girlfriend of mine and was the officiant of Tony and Domenica's wedding.

"You're going to Michele's?" Domenica asks me.

"Yes, that's the plan. I have an early flight, and Michele has a driver who can take me."

"That sounds good."

~~~~~~

> Sometimes, flying feels too godlike to be attained
> by man. Sometimes, the world from above seems
> too beautiful, too wonderful, too distant for
> human eyes to see. . . .
>
> —CHARLES A. LINDBERGH

~~~~~~

The Frenzels are stocking the refrigerator. Domenica and I are speaking in code. She knows my nerves before a flight.

"I'm sure it will be fine," I tell her.

"You mean that, don't you?" she asks, antennae tingling.

"Yes. It's the day before flying and I have no jitters to speak of."

"Mommy, that's great!" Domenica is excited for me.

Watching my daughter with her new daughter, my first grandchild, I am filled with a sense of expansion and hope. Watching Serafina fuss, watching Domenica soothe her, my fear of flying feels miles away. It's hard to imagine I ever had any hesitation about getting on a plane when this is where it would take me, and it occurs to me that I might be experiencing an answered prayer.

"Thank you," I pray. "Thank you."

Discover Julia Cameron's Creative Kingdom

To order, call 1-800-788-6262 or visit our website at www.penguin.com

BOOKS IN *THE ARTIST'S WAY* SERIES

The Artist's Way
ISBN   978-1-58542-147-3 (hardcover)
ISBN   978-1-58542-146-6 (trade paper)
ISBN   978-0-14-305825-0 (audio, CDs)

Walking in This World
ISBN   978-1-58542-261-6 (trade paper)

Finding Water
ISBN   978-1-58542-463-4 (hardcover)
ISBN   978-1-58542-777-2 (trade paper)

The Artist's Way Workbook
ISBN   978-1-58542-533-4 (trade paper)

The Artist's Way Morning Pages Journal
ISBN   978-0-87477-886-1 (trade paper)

The Complete Artist's Way
ISBN   978-1-58542-630-0 (hardcover)

The Artist's Way Every Day
ISBN   978-1-58542-747-5 (trade paper)

The Artist's Date Book
ISBN   978-0-87477-653-9 (trade paper)

Inspirations: Meditations from
The Artist's Way
ISBN   978-1-58542-102-2 (trade paper)

OTHER BOOKS ON CREATIVITY

The Right to Write
ISBN   978-1-58542-009-4 (trade paper)

The Sound of Paper
ISBN   978-1-58542-354-5 (trade paper)

The Writing Diet
ISBN   978-1-58542-698-0 (trade paper)

The Vein of Gold
ISBN   978-0-87477-879-3 (trade paper)

How to Avoid Making Art (or Anything
Else You Enjoy)
ISBN   978-1-58542-438-2 (trade paper)

The Writer's Life: Insights from The Right
to Write
ISBN   978-1-58542-103-9 (trade paper)

Supplies: A Troubleshooting Guide for
Creative Difficulties
ISBN   978-1-58542-212-8 (trade paper)

The Creative Life: True Tales of Inspiration
ISBN   978-1-58542-824-3 (hardcover)

PRAYER BOOKS

Answered Prayers
ISBN   978-1-58542-351-4 (trade paper)

Heart Steps
ISBN   978-0-87477-899-1 (trade paper)

Blessings
ISBN   978-0-87477-906-6 (trade paper)

Transitions
ISBN   978-0-87477-995-0 (trade paper)

Prayers to the Great Creator
ISBN   978-1-58542-682-9 (hardcover)
ISBN   978-1-58542-778-9 (trade paper)

BOOKS ON SPIRITUALITY

Faith and Will
ISBN   978-1-58542-714-7 (hardcover)

Prayers from a Nonbeliever
ISBN   978-1-58542-213-5 (hardcover)

Letters to a Young Artist
ISBN   978-1-58542-409-2 (hardcover)

God Is No Laughing Matter
ISBN   978-1-58542-128-2 (trade paper)

MEMOIR

Floor Sample: A Creative Memoir
ISBN   978-1-58542-494-8 (hardcover)
ISBN   978-158542-557-0 (trade paper)

Watch Julia Cameron on Tarcher Talks @ www.penguin.com/tarchertalks

GIVE THE GIFT OF
CREATIVE INSPIRATION

Two *Artist's Way* gift sets are now available to mark the 20th anniversary of this international bestseller.

A $75 value, for just $59

978-1-58542-927-1
The Artist's Way: Creative Kingdom Collection is a gorgeous box set that contains Julia Cameron's most essential tools—*The Artist's Way, The Artist's Way Workbook, The Artist's Way Morning Pages Journal,* and the *Artist's Way* audiobook. The *Kingdom Collection* offers everything an aspiring writer or artist needs to fully experience Cameron's life-changing creativity program.

978-1-58542-928-8 · $29.95
The Artist's Way Starter Kit includes Cameron's two most important tools—*The Artist's Way* and *The Artist's Way Morning Pages Journal*—attractively shrink-wrapped together with a belly band. This *Starter Kit* is the perfect entry point for those who want to start unblocking their creativity!

For more information, visit www.JuliaCameronLive.com
or www.tarcherbooks.com/juliacameron.